EMBODYING A THEOLOGY OF MINISTRY AND LEADERSHIP

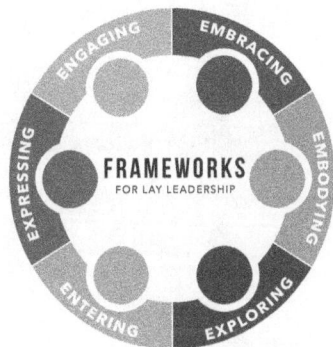

Rob A. Fringer, series editor

EMBODYING A THEOLOGY OF MINISTRY AND LEADERSHIP

Bruce G. Allder

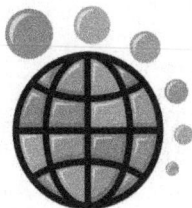

Global Nazarene Publications

ISBN 978-1-56344-873-7

Global Nazarene Publication
Lenexa, Kansas (USA)

Copyright © 2018
Bruce G. Allder

DIGITAL PRINTING

TABLE OF CONTENTS

FRAMEWORKS
FOR LAY LEADERSHIP

Scripture tells us that believers are "a royal priesthood" (1 Peter 2:9). This means that all Christians, in one form or another, are called into places of ministry and leadership. Not only is this a great privilege, it is also a great responsibility. Men and women desiring to serve in church leadership in some capacity undergo basic training to assure that they understand the foundations of the Christian faith and of our Nazarene identity. This includes a deepening knowledge and appreciation of Scripture, Theology, Ministry, Mission, History, and Holiness. *Frameworks for Lay Leadership* is a series of six books designed to do just that—equip lay leaders for ministry in the Church, whether local, district, or general. These books have the greatest impact when they are read, processed, applied, and contextualised in partnership with a qualified mentor.

Welcome to this journey of transformation!

ENGAGING THE STORY OF GOD

EXPLORING A WESLEYAN THEOLOGY

EMBODYING A THEOLOGY OF MINISTRY AND LEADERSHIP

ENTERING THE MISSION OF GOD

EXPRESSING A NAZARENE IDENTITY

EMBRACING A DOCTRINE OF HOLINESS

CHAPTER 1

INTRODUCTION

I remember coming home from church one day having heard one of the best sermons of my life about responding to God's call to ministry. The thought suddenly struck me, "How in the world would I live out what I had just heard?" It sounded so good at the time; yet, when all the hype was gone, I was left overwhelmed with the enormity of the challenge and not sure how to implement the insights gained. I may not be the only one who felt this after enjoying the challenge of a great sermon. However, I have learned that it is possible to hear from God and respond in such a way that I live differently and embrace a life of service. In the following pages, I will give some pointers to living out an amazing life-calling. My prayer is that it will set you on a path of life transformation through discovery and growth.

We begin by unpacking the title of this book starting with the word *ministry*. What comes to mind when you hear this term? Perhaps you think of a pastor of a local church who does the work of ministry, or of someone who dresses up in robes that looks positively Mediaeval. What about the person who conducts funerals and visits the sick in hospital? Perhaps it is the person (man or woman) who stands behind the pulpit each Sunday. Nevertheless, this term, *ministry*, is not about a person but the action of serving. Anyone who seeks to serve others in a way that honours Christ is doing *ministry*. At its core, ministry means serving and working for the benefit of the one being served.[1] We can all be involved, whether we are the formal leaders of a congregation or members of the faith community with no formal education or training in Bible or theology. In serving, "like living stones, [we] are being built into a spiritual house to be a holy priesthood, offering spiritual sacrifices acceptable to

God through Jesus Christ" (1 Peter 2:5). These powerful words are written to all Christians, not just the leaders of the church. This inclusive nature of serving (ministry) is often referred to as the *priesthood of all believers* and is an important biblical concept. All believers must remember that regardless of their vocation, they are still called to serve Christ by serving others.[2]

Leadership is another vexing term because there are so many differing ideas about what it is and how it should look. When you hear the term *leader*, do you think of a person with great authority or public influence? Do you think about political leaders of the past who have seemed to lead nations? Perhaps you think of those who speak for a vast number of people in times of crisis, for example, Winston Churchill, Martin Luther King Jr., or Nelson Mandela. Undoubtedly, these people were leaders, but leadership is much more than this highly visible, dramatic display. Leadership is ultimately influence,[3] and godly leadership is "leading people onto God's agenda."[4] All of us can be influencers in our own quiet way, which, according to this definition, means we can all be leaders. Before you protest at this assertion, think of people with whom you have regular contact and of the ways they impact your life. The reverse is also true; you impact them too. Welcome to the place of leadership! If we are impacting others, the important question for each of us to ask ourselves is "What kind of impact do I want to have?" or "What kind of influencer do I want to be?"[5] As with the term *ministry*, the term *leadership* encompasses a wider view than perhaps first thought.

Theology is a word that often carries with it connotations of deep thinking and perhaps thinking that few can fathom. However, the simple definition of theology is the study (*logos*) of God (*theos*). Most of us do this regularly, even if we are not doing it formally. A theology of ministry and leadership is the study of ministry and leadership in light of our understanding and belief in God and within the context of the Kingdom of God. Here, theology seeks to address such questions as: "What is God's agenda for ministry and leadership?"; "How would God want us to minister and lead?"; "Where is God in the activity of ministry and leadership?"

Finally, the term *embodying* brings an important aspect to our exploration of ministry and leadership. Embodiment means the physical expression of what otherwise might be a theoretical idea. This has profound implications for the "why" and the "how" of ministry and leadership. The term *incarnation* similarly captures the physicality and practical expression of living out the principles of ministry and leadership. Credibility for ministry and leadership is found not in how well we can articulate the principles, but in how well we live out those principles, particularly in the light of Scripture. Rather than pointing to a discussion or an idea, embodiment means we point to a person and their life of doing. For example, Jesus says, "anyone who has seen me has seen the Father. How can you say, 'Show us the Father'? Don't you believe that I am in the Father, and that the Father is in me?" (John 14:9b-10a).

With this understanding of the title, we now move into a deeper consideration of the aspects of ministry and leadership. Firstly, we will explore the *being* within ministry and leadership; who we are as a person and what God is ultimately doing in and with us in his world. Secondly, we will explore biblical images for ministry and leadership; this is God's work in which we are seeking to cooperate and in which we should be guided by his Word. Thirdly, we will examine the *doing* of ministry and leadership; the tasks of ministry and leadership will help us set a few parameters. Fourthly, and perhaps most importantly, we will explore a way of putting the *being* and the *doing* of ministry and leadership together under the rubric of *incarnational leadership*. This is where we seek to embody the principles of the earlier sections.

QUESTIONS FOR REFLECTION

1. What is your response to 1 Peter 2:5 and the idea of the "priesthood of all believers"? Why do you think this concept is important?

2. What kind of leader do you think God is calling you to be in your local context and why?

3. What scares you about *doing* theology? Why do you think it is important to develop a theology of ministry and leadership?

CHAPTER 2

BEING **IN MINISTRY AND LEADERSHIP**

As Christians, we are called into a future designed by God. Being in sync with this future is the prerequisite for effective ministry and leadership. This purpose is not something abstract or unknowable. There is a particularity to this goal and purpose that is both vivid and definable. For the Christian, the purpose is Christ, who is the embodiment of our calling.[6] In other words, we are designed to *be* and *become* Christlike.

Our Ultimate Purpose

Effective Christian ministry and leadership is never simply a job. It springs from who we are as persons and, more importantly, who we are as followers of Jesus. This raises the question of identity and of our connection with our Creator. Understanding this connection begins with finding our true purpose in life as human beings. Augustine said, "You have made us for yourself, O Lord, and our heart is restless until it rests in You."[7] Prior to his conversion, Augustine was a renowned teacher of public speaking. Even with all the trappings that were associated with the royal courts of the Roman Empire, Augustine was ever restless. However, after he converted to Christianity, he was transformed. Augustine embraced what he saw as his originally intended vocation as a God-created human being, worshipping God alone.

Instead of embracing the vocation of worshipping God alone, humanity rejected God and turned to the worship of idols. In so doing, humanity became enslaved to the very things over which God had given us dominion.[8] That is the bad news. But in Christ, we are beckoned back to our original vocation and calling. We are made by God and for God, and "to be truly and fully human, we need to 'find' ourselves in relationship to the One who made us and for whom we are made. The gospel is the way we learn to be human."[9] The Genesis account outlines this human vocation:

> Then God said: "Let us make mankind in our image, in our likeness, so that they may rule over the fish in the sea and the birds in the sky, over the livestock and all the wild animals, and over all the creatures that move along the ground." So, God created mankind in his own image, in the image of God he created them; male and female he created them. (Genesis 1:26-27)

Genuine Christian spirituality understands humanity as beings created in the image of God and participating with God in a fallen creation, which God intends to fully redeem. "Such a life of loving union with God results in Christlikeness—wholeness in the image of God. This is not a self-referenced, self-contained, achievement independent from our life with others in creation. ... [This] is a process of being formed in the image of Christ for the sake of the world."[10] Before we can get to *doing*, we need to *be* on the journey to Christlikeness. This journey requires us to be a follower of Jesus.

There are barriers along the way as we seek to follow Jesus and become Christlike. These barriers are not insurmountable, but knowing the hindrances along the way will help us. Klaus Issler outlines five of these barriers as they relate to our journey to Christlikeness. They are based on a review of the parable of the sower (Matthew 13:1-23).

- *Dismissive Barrier* (resistance to truths that seem impossible to us)
- *Discrepancy Barrier* (professed values that are not character deep)
- *Distracted Barrier* (a lifestyle slowly drifting off course)

• *Disconnected Barrier* (not regularly abiding in Jesus)

• *Distressed Barrier* (an initial moment of troubling emotional stress that is not addressed and becomes debilitating, excessive worry)[11]

To overcome these barriers, a whole-hearted commitment to the journey towards Christlikeness is required. The good news is that this is not a "think positive" or "I think I can make it" mentality that needs to be generated in our own energy. The restlessness that is part of our humanity is instilled in us by our Creator. That is to say, seeking and hungering after that which will truly satisfy is inherent. As the writer of Ecclesiastes writes, God has "set eternity in the human heart" (Ecclesiastes 3:11). Furthermore, Jesus gives us good news when he says, "Blessed are those who hunger and thirst for righteousness, for they will be filled" (Matthew 5:6).

James K. A. Smith describes this hungering as a pursuit. This pursuit is not simply to know something or believe in some goal. Rather, it is what we long for, desire, and want ultimately.[12] It is what we love! It grabs us at the deepest level possible, and this opens the possibilities for transformation. Think for a moment of the barriers that can hinder that love. Discipleship (what we often define as the process and journey toward Christlikeness) is more about shaping the orientation of our heart (our loves) than it is about gaining more information for head knowledge.

This suggests a way forward in our journey of being a disciple of Jesus. The agenda for shaping our *being* is found in our times of worship.

> Christian worship … is essentially a counter-formation to those rival liturgies we are often immersed in, cultural practices that covertly capture our loves and longings, miscalibrating them, orienting us to rival versions of the good life. This is why worship is at the heart of discipleship. We can't counter the power of cultural liturgies with didactic information poured into our intellects. We can't recalibrate the heart from the top down, through merely informational measures. The orientation of the heart happens from the bottom up, through the formation of our habits of desire. Learning to love (God) takes practice.[13]

It is here that we must make an important distinction. The knowing that we speak of in the shaping of our *being* is not knowing about God in Jesus Christ; rather, it is knowing in a deeper way. For example, I have been married for over 40 years, and I know my wife well. I not only know a lot about her—what she looks like, her interests and hobbies, her talents and abilities, and so forth—I also know her as a person. I know her likes and loves, the way she thinks (well most of the time!); I can predict what she will say about something because I know her values and how her life experiences have shaped her. This knowing is a life journey, ever-deepening, full of surprises, joys, and challenges. This latter knowing is our goal in knowing God. The interesting thing about this kind of knowing is that, just as I have been influenced and shaped as a husband and as a person by my increasing knowing of my wife, so we are shaped by our increasing knowing of God: Father, Son, and Holy Spirit. This knowing is relationship based and is mutually engaging.

Character Formation and Spiritual Formation

The journey of change at the core of our being is often termed spiritual formation or character formation. There is a debate about whether these two terms should be used interchangeably. In one sense, the term *character formation* is preferable, because the term *spiritual formation* can sometimes imply a dichotomy of spirit and matter, soul and body.[14] This implication is unfortunate because the formation that God is doing in us is as much about how we respond in everyday life as it is about discerning a life that is less material. The two are indissolubly linked. We cannot have one without the other.

> We know that we have come to know him if we keep his commands. Whoever says, "I know him," but does not do what he commands is a liar, and the truth is not in that person. But if anyone obeys his word, love for God is truly made complete in them. This is how we know we are in him: Whoever claims to live in him must live as Jesus did. (1 John 2:3-6)

On the other hand, the term *spiritual formation* suggests more than what we see and touch. There is a dimension to every relationship that is expressed spiritually, in non-material ways. There is a sense that "we know more than we can say."[15] This is sometimes labelled *emotional learning*, and while this learning may lack words, it will always feels true. This learning is not immutable, but it does point to a powerful non-material part of our being.

Given that we centre our *being* in a recalibration of our heart toward God and relationship with him, it is essential to have a teachable spirit. Discipleship is not just about following Jesus; it is about learning in the way the first disciples learned from Jesus; it is about learning along the way.[16] We should avoid the temptation to run another seminar or Bible study and think that this is discipleship. Too often this moves back into simply accumulating knowledge instead of *being* or life transformation. Core to this *being* is a disposition of humility as we journey together.

> There is a story about a Dean of a school of theology who came to a Zen master to ask him about Zen. Nan-in, the Zen master, served him tea. He poured his visitor's cup full, then kept pouring. The Dean watched the overflow until he could no longer restrain himself. "It is over-full. No more will go in." "Like this cup," Nan-in said, "you are full of your own opinions and speculations. How can I teach you Zen unless you first empty your cup?"[17]

I'm sure you get the picture. Humility is emptying our cup of our own opinions and speculations to hear what God has to say. This relationship is a two-way street and we need to listen at least as much as we talk, probably more.

How, then, are we to be attentive to what God has to say? This is where the spiritual disciplines come into play. There is some *doing* in order to *be* in the process of formation, and this journey will not necessarily be easy. Paul's words give us both encouragement and challenge:

> Therefore, since we have been justified through faith, we have peace with God through our Lord Jesus Christ, through whom we have gained access by faith into this grace in which we now stand. And we boast in the hope of the glory of God. Not only so, but we also glory in our sufferings, because we know that suffering produces

perseverance; perseverance, character; and character, hope. And hope does not put us to shame, because God's love has been poured out into our hearts through the Holy Spirit, who has been given to us. (Romans 5:1-5)

The Spiritual Disciplines

John Wesley taught that God's grace is unearned, but that we are not to be idle waiting to experience that grace. By engaging in the spiritual disciplines (what Wesley called the "means of grace"), we are providing ways for God to continue to work in our lives. These disciplines have been categorised as follows:

Works of Piety

- *Individual Practices*: reading, meditating and studying the Scriptures, prayer, fasting, regularly attending worship, healthy living, and sharing our faith with others

- *Communal Practices*: regularly sharing in the sacraments, Christian conferencing (accountability to one another), and Bible study

Works of Mercy

- *Individual Practices*: doing good works, visiting the sick, visiting those in prison, feeding the hungry, and giving generously to those in need

- *Communal Practices*: seeking justice, ending oppression and discrimination, addressing the needs of the poor[18]

It is the works of piety that, initially, are fertile ground for active listening to God. Regular, intentional involvement in these practices, so they become habits, is an important part of practical piety for the Christian. For example, communal worship not only shapes our mind but, moreover, it reshapes our imaginations and our practices and enables us to be the Body of Christ ministering to one another and from there to our world.[19] Is it any wonder that the writer of Hebrews says, "let us consider how we may spur one another on toward love and good deeds, not giving up meeting together, as some are in the habit of doing, but encouraging one another" (Hebrews 10:24-25)?

The embrace of the Scriptures is foundational to our listening to God and to character formation. Systematic, frequent immersion in the message of Scripture will provide the scaffolding for understanding the story of God and how our story can become part of his story. There are numerous ways to embrace reading and listening to Scripture as part of our life, three that can be especially helpful.

Firstly, there is the daily devotional reading of Scripture. Many guides are available, and it only takes a few minutes each day to read the designated selection. Choose a set time each day (often associated with another regular daily activity such as eating breakfast) when you can habitually take a few moments to read and pray. This is not the time for in depth study, but simply to begin a conversation with God that will continue throughout the day. Ideally, this is done early to set the tone for the rest of the day.

Secondly, find the lectionary readings for each Sunday and read these Scriptures daily prior to the scheduled Sunday.[20] Lectionary readings are a systematic set of Bible readings that have been developed over many years by various Christian denominations to be used in public worship. The goal of these readings is to cover the message of the whole Bible over a period of three years. The selections follow the Christian Calendar (Advent, Christmas, Lent, Easter, and so on). Over a period of several months, a wide range of the Scripture (not just our favourites) is covered, and the reader begins to understand the full story of what God has done, is doing, and will do in his world. The story is not monochromatic, and an amazing variety is on display through this process. Alternatively, rather than commit to readings from a variety of places in Scripture, some commit to reading through the entire Bible in a year. While the quantity to be read is substantial, it can also give a fuller picture of the story of God.

Thirdly, use the process of *divine reading* (*lectio divina*) as a way of reading and praying the Scriptures.[21] This approach seeks to read the Bible in a way that promotes communion with God. While particularly effective as a group exercise, it can be done individually as well. The process is simple. Take a moment to quiet your heart and then select a passage of Scripture (often from the Gospels or an Epistle, five to ten verses in length) and read it aloud. Think of a word or phrase that stood out to you as you heard yourself read. Think about that word or phrase and reflect on the insight gained. Then re-read the passage in the light of what you have just thought about. Consider what just happened and see what deeper insight you have because of the re-reading. Take a moment to speak to God in prayer based upon this reading. It might be that you read the passage of Scripture again another two or three times as you tune your ear to hear what God is saying to you. This process has a way of slowing us down, removing the "noises" that makes it hard to hear the voice of God, and drawing us into the task of listening.

Having listened well to God through his word, we can then respond in obedience to the voice of God. This is at the heart of character development and the essence of obedience is integrity. In the words of 1 Peter 1:22-23: "Now that you have purified yourselves by obeying the truth so that you have sincere love for each other, love one another deeply, from the heart. For you have been born again, not of perishable seed, but of imperishable, through the living and enduring word of God."

Integrity is about "conforming reality to our words—in other words, keeping promises and fulfilling expectations."[22] Stephen Covey states three components to integrity: *congruency* (where a person acts according to their values), *humility* (a person is more concerned about what is right than in being right; embracing new truth, rather than defending an opinion), and *courage* (the ability to do the right thing even when it is difficult).[23] As we practice these disciplines our character is formed and we become more authentic followers of Christ. It starts with an integrated, authentic self and ripples out into all our relationships, into our church, and into our society.

Trust is central to this process of growth. Do we trust God? Do we trust others? Am I a person that others can trust? Trust is *the* virtue of ministry.[24] In ministry and leadership, we must learn to trust others and this trust must be in and inspired by God. Trust is comprehensive (see Figure 1);[25] it relates directly to both the interior and exterior life of those in ministry and leadership. The interior life requires courage and intentional cultivation because it is not seen by others. We could be tempted to become lax in the disciplines that cultivate the interior life because it is so private and because of the personal costs of time, energy, and self-discipline required for such cultivation. It is not an easy road to adjust personal world views and values, especially those that have been held for many years. Listening well to the Holy Spirit and following the Spirit's leading is sometimes countercultural.

Brené Brown has a practical challenge in her *Anatomy of Trust* under the acronym "BRAVING."[26]

- *B*oundaries – respecting the other person's boundaries and having my own

- *Reliability* – being both reliable and authentic

- *Accountability* – owning my own mistakes, apologising and making amends

- *Vault* – what I share with you, you hold in confidence, and I do the same for you

- *Integrity* – choosing courage over comfort, what's right over what's fun, easy, or fast

- *Non-judgement & reciprocity* – offering and asking for help

- *Generous* – believing the best in the other even when they disappoint

Often, a leader can be perceived as doing a great job according to external measures of ministry success. However, if we are not cultivating the spiritual life, our outward actions will eventually reveal our emptiness or even our darkness. This is the criticism that Jesus made of many of the religious leaders of his day; they focussed on the externals to the detriment of the interior life.

> Woe to you, teachers of the law and Pharisees, you hypocrites! You are like whitewashed tombs, which look beautiful on the outside but on the inside, are full of the bones of the dead and everything

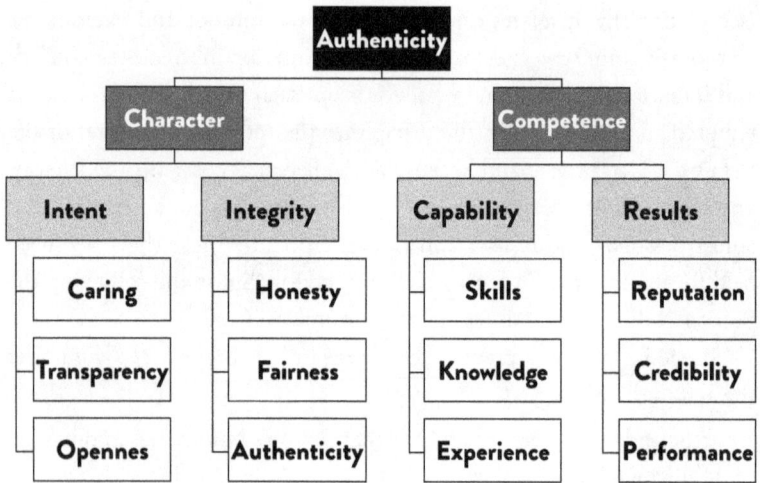

Figure 1

unclean. In the same way, on the outside you appear to people as righteous but on the inside, you are full of hypocrisy and wickedness. (Matthew 23:27-28)

To make the decision to follow Christ is just the beginning of the journey of growth and development. To assume that this growth will happen automatically is like bringing a child into the world and expecting the infant to feed himself or herself. An effective way to cultivate and deepen our relationship with God is by holding ourselves accountable to a small group of fellow disciples or another individual. Wesley was aware of our tendency to take the easy way in our spiritual development. He is well known for his system of small groups to counter this. It is this system that helped the Methodist movement to cultivate effective disciples and, moreover, to keep them growing.

Wesley's class meetings were a subdivision of the larger Methodist Society. However, to be a regular attender at the Society a person needed to be a regular participant in a class meeting. It was at the class meeting that the focus was almost exclusively on the alteration of behaviour.

There was no room here for lecturing or preaching; the emphasis was clearly on present and personal growth, presided over, not by a professional trainer, but by a fellow seeker. … Not only were the class meetings mixed groupings according to sex, they were also heterogeneous in terms of age, social standing, and spiritual readiness. … Wesley visualised the class meeting as the point of entry for most initiates into Methodism, and he wanted the entry group to be a warm fellowship of fellow strugglers, representing a broad cross-section of Methodism.[27]

What is particularly telling is the role of the leaders of these class meetings. Once a hymn was sung to start the class meeting, the leader would give a personal testimony of their own spiritual condition, which set the tone for the rest of the participants to do likewise.[28] A transparent inner personal life shared in community was the prerequisite of the leader, and in fact, of each member of the class meeting. This became an important part of the accountability process built within the worshipping community from the very beginning of a person's contact with the faith community.

There were other accountability groups within the Methodist system that related to other leaders and those with greater spiritual maturity (e.g. "Bands" and "Select Societies"). However, the class leaders were the fledgling pastors in the Methodist organisational hierarchy. It was understood that they carried pastoral oversight of the group and were regarded as being on the first rung of the leadership ladder.[29] Clearly, *being* was a prerequisite for learning to lead.

With intentional development of character, there is a consequent expression of the life we live in Christ. The apostle Paul speaks of the *fruit of the Spirit*—fruit being the evidence of the work of the Holy Spirit in the life of the believer. "The fruit of the Spirit is love, joy, peace, forbearance, kindness, goodness, faithfulness, gentleness and self-control" (Galatians 5:22-23). The "fruit" is cultivated through the practice of the spiritual disciplines and walking in obedience to the promptings of the Holy Spirit.

However, we have core values that directly influence our actions. We hold these tightly and they reflect what we truly care about in life. It is these values that create decision-making pathways that help us reflect our true selves.[30] It is extremely beneficial to identify these core values as they guide us in our personal priorities, ministry commitments, goals, and conflict management.[31] For Wesley, the love of people appears to have been a core value that drove his life and ministry. Wesley began with people and their needs; he followed the migration of people so that there would be ministry where people lived; and he focused on serving, especially remembering the poor.[32]

Placing such a high value on people had a profound impact on the shape of Wesley's ministry. Even when such a value drove him into conducting ministry in ways he was personally uncomfortable with, he proceeded. For example, Wesley appeared to go through significant personal anguish as he began preaching in the fields, away from church buildings; he was after all a staunch churchman. While there were several external motivators for Wesley's field-preaching, including the repeated requests from his contemporary, George Whitefield, "it was the internal invasion of a sanctifying God that nurtured an empathetic love in Wesley that drove him to the fields."[33] Wesley was apparently willing to do what was necessary to reach people with the Gospel. However, this practicality was not mere pragmatism, or doing whatever works. His practice was still within the bounds of a theological position informed by his empathy.

Here is an important lesson for the practice of ministry. Core values should not always be rigidly applied; there is flexibility. Some people pride themselves on having many strongly held convictions that become values in their own right. The essential question to answer is whether the conviction is a value or simply a preferred way of doing something. If many convictions or preferred ways of doing things become core values, then we can develop an inflexibility in our ministry and leadership. As leaders, we must be careful not to justify our personal way of doing things by claiming they are biblical or theologically mandated. Trying to claim the moral high ground on such preferences is a sure way to undermine our own integrity; it is essentially a selfish orientation. The challenge is to ensure that our core values are reflections of biblical values that are Spirit inspired. Keeping the core values to a small number, but providing a multitude of ways of expressing them, gives rise to flexibility in actions. Core values remain stable, but their expressions may vary enormously.

The Apostle Peter is a great example of one who had to adjust a firmly held conviction when he realised that it was a cultural understanding and not consistent with the Gospel. Acts 10 records the incident where Peter had a dream about clean and unclean food. Peter learned that God was declaring some things clean that Peter, because of his Jewish heritage, had thought unclean. Moments after the dream, Peter was urged to visit the home of a Gentile. As a Jew, he would ordinarily decline such an invitation. Nevertheless, because of the dream, he accepted, and the result was that a great many Gentiles accepted Christ as their Saviour. Peter came to understand that the Gospel was not just for the Jewish people. Peter's practices needed to change according to the new values he was adopting; Kingdom values!

We might easily read over this passage without fully comprehending the immense emotional and spiritual energy required by Peter to make such a radical shift. This change struck at the core of who Peter was as a person. Every fibre of his being would have been screaming, "This isn't right!" However, in his whole-hearted love for Christ, he adjusted his values and life priorities. That is to say, he saw that a change needed to be made. We know this was not easy because later he was reprimanded by the Apostle Paul for drifting back into his old exclusive ways (Galatians 2:11-21). The transformation of core values requires the life-transforming involvement of the Holy Spirit. This is a demonstration of integrity— having our actions reflect our words.

When Things Go Wrong

We must admit that sometimes leadership gets it wrong. We find ourselves doing something other than reflecting Christlikeness. Illegitimate sources of influence can have us building on a human foundation rather than a godly one. The selfish use of a leadership position, the use of coercive power, or an emphasis on a forceful personality that does not listen well, are such examples. If these are our sources for influence, we stand on very shaky ground. We can be tempted to use these sources because we are impatient for results, think we know best, or have learned to rely solely on ourselves. It is a tragedy for the church community if most of our actions do not need the Holy Spirit to empower or provide. "Some spiritual leaders try to be more committed. What they need is to be more submitted."[34] We can "organise" God out of our ministry and leadership when we stop intentionally listening to him.

Prayer is an integral part of listening well to God. Prayer is a two-way conversation with our heavenly Father. Why do we pray? Firstly, prayer shows our dependency upon God. As we pray, we humbly acknowledge that we do not have all the answers. Secondly, prayer gives us the opportunity to listen and to pick up on God's agenda. I remember a time in my first pastorate in Australia when I sat at my desk having visited all the people in the small congregation. My sermons were prepared for the next few weeks, and I wondered what I was going to do with my time as pastor. I was young and inexperienced. Then, it was almost like I heard a voice say to me, "Get out of your chair and go walk the community." I did that, not knowing what I was supposed to see or to look for. But as I prayerfully walked the streets of the local community, I found a small community service organisation that needed help with personnel. That discovery transformed my ministry and that of the local church. A wonderful opportunity for service to the wider community opened through a partnership with several Baptists and community minded people. In hind sight, even though it felt strange to walk around not really knowing what I was looking for, I was listening to God's agenda.

QUESTIONS FOR REFLECTION

1. What do you see as humanities ultimate purpose and why? How is this purpose connected to our being created in the image of God?

2. Looking at Klaus Issler's five barriers to Christlikeness, which ones do you struggle most with and why do you think that is? What can you do to move beyond these barriers?

3. Why is involvement in corporate worship important in our character formation? Is this priority reflected in your life? What might need to change to ensure that it becomes or remains a priority?

4. Look at the list of spiritual disciplines listed. Which of these have you practiced, and which would you like to try? List ways that several of these disciplines can be incorporated into your life currently.

5. How would you define integrity and how important do you think it is to ministry and leadership? Are there any areas of your own life and ministry where your words and actions are not in line? What are some steps you can take to bring them in line?

6. Think of someone in ministry that you trust. What makes this person trustworthy in your eyes? What intentional steps can you take to cultivate trusting relationships within the community you serve?

7. Prayerfully consider your personal core values? What makes them core to you? Does anything need to be added or subtracted from this list? Why? Consider leading your church through this same consideration about its core values.

CHAPTER 3

A BIBLICAL PERSPECTIVE OF MINISTRY AND LEADERSHIP

In the previous section, we explored *being* as the ground for ministry and leadership. Here, it is worth examining what the Bible says about this important topic before moving to the *doing* of ministry and leadership. The four areas of focus are: the shepherd as a biblical motif for ministry and leadership; the servant as a biblical mode of ministry and leadership; the incarnation as a biblical understanding of *being* in ministry and leadership; and the empowering of others as a biblical mandate for ministry and leadership.

Shepherd as Motif for Ministry and Leadership

The Shepherd motif appears throughout Scripture at critical times in the grand narrative of God's working in his world with his people. The setting for much of the biblical literature may be significantly different from what most of us experience today. The biblical culture was predominantly rural and agricultural imagery was one of the best ways of explaining ideas and principles. This makes the image of the shepherd particularly appropriate for exploring the motif of leadership. In the Old Testament, Kings were referred to as shepherds (Jeremiah 23:1-4; Ezekiel 34), as were the other leaders of Israel, including the religious leaders. While many leaders were referred to as bad shepherds, Psalm 23 is well known for speaking about God as the Good Shepherd.

I remember driving a quiet road in the sheep country of Australia and coming across a farmer sitting on a quad bike in the middle of the road. His hundreds of sheep wandered along the roadside. A trusty sheep dog was nearby, and the sheep were being driven to pasture five kilometres down the road. There was no hurry; but there were clear expectations by the farmer that he would forcefully drive the sheep to the next pasture.

This could not be further from the imagery that a person in biblical days would understand. Firstly, the number of sheep supervised by the shepherd would have been vastly smaller; it would have been small enough for the shepherd to recognise each of his own sheep and for the sheep to recognise the shepherd's voice and to follow after him. At night, the shepherd might cooperate with other shepherds and gather several small flocks together and create a make-shift corral to keep out wild animals. One of the shepherds would then lie across the entrance to sleep so that nothing could get in or out without the shepherd knowing.

Given this very different understanding of the role of the shepherd, the following passage of Scripture makes more sense.

> Very truly I tell you Pharisees, anyone who does not enter the sheep pen by the gate, but climbs in by some other way, is a thief and a robber. The one who enters by the gate is the shepherd of the sheep. The gatekeeper opens the gate for him, and the sheep listen to his voice. He calls his own sheep by name and leads them out. When he has brought out all of his own, he goes ahead of them, and his sheep follow him because they know his voice. (John 10:1-4)

Good shepherds are intimately involved with their sheep, know them well, and provide safety. They nourish their sheep and give direction by leading them (rather than driving them). Despite all the negative comments about poor shepherding (poor leadership) given in the Scriptures, Jesus declares himself to be the Good Shepherd (John 10:11).

In John 21:15-19, there is a powerful account of Christ's forgiveness and restoration of Peter for his three denials; this is combined with the commission to feed Christ's sheep. Peter is being asked to be an *under shepherd* to the Good Shepherd. The Apostle Peter later writes:

To the elders among you, I appeal as a fellow elder and witness of Christ's sufferings who also will share in the glory to be revealed: Be shepherds of God's flock that is under your care, watching over them—not because you must, but because you are willing, as God wants you to be; not pursuing dishonest gain, but eager to serve; not lording it over those entrusted to you, but being examples to the flock. (1 Peter 5:1-3)

The implications for leadership are both clear and profound. We are entrusted to positively influence (perhaps lead) a group of people with whom we have contact. We are to be stewards, taking care of what has been entrusted to us, rather than "owning" the influence we have with people. This is not a "right to rule," but a privileged gift to be treasured and stewarded.

Servanthood as a Mode for Ministry and Leadership

The servanthood of Jesus is plain to see in both his words and his actions.

Jesus called them together and said, "You know that those who are regarded as rulers of the Gentiles lord it over them, and their high officials exercise authority over them. Not so with you. Instead, whoever wants to become great among you must be your servant, and whoever wants to be first must be slave of all. For even the Son of Man did not come to be served, but to serve, and to give his life as a ransom for many." (Mark 10:42-45)

Prior to offering up himself on the cross, Jesus demonstrated this servant-like attitude by washing the disciples' feet. This task was a common courtesy offered by a host to arriving guests, usually done by one of the lower ranked people in the household, maybe even a slave. Nevertheless, Jesus did not often conform to worldly social constructs of status. Instead, he made clear through this humble demonstration that servanthood was a core component of ministry and leadership.

"Do you understand what I have done for you?" he asked them. "You call me 'Teacher' and 'Lord', and rightly so, for that is what I am. Now that I, your Lord and Teacher, have washed your feet, you also should wash one another's feet. I have set you an example that you should do as I have done for you. Very truly I tell you, no servant is greater than his master, nor is a messenger greater than the one who sent him." (John 13:12b-16)

In the Old Testament, kings were thought of in terms of servants of Yahweh. They were called to be leaders who guided the people toward God and his ways. However, these earthly kings often failed, many using their power for selfish gain. Jesus, on the other hand, as the true King of Israel (and of the whole world), brought together servanthood and leadership. Therefore, biblically, we can speak of *servant leadership*, even though their union appears quite counter-intuitive.

While this terminology has become a part of secular leadership conversations, it is a relatively recent phenomenon. It was Robert Greenleaf in 1970 who initiated scholarly interest in *servant leadership*. While writing to a secular audience, Greenleaf's statement is apropos: "The best test [of servant leadership] is: do those served grow as persons; do they while being served, become healthier, wiser, freer, more autonomous, more likely themselves to become servants?"[35] We could add, "and become more Christlike in the process." Servanthood is desiring the best for others, even above ourselves. On this basis, we do not set the agenda, nor the interpretive lens through which we view leadership and ministry activity. These are set by Christ's example and teaching.

Incarnation as *Being* in Ministry and Leadership

From a Biblical point of view our calling to ministry and leadership in Christ is a lived experience and not just a job to be done. Like Jesus, we must be incarnational. The Apostle Paul's words in Philippians 2:6-8 highlight the sacrifice of Jesus's incarnation and the depths of his love for humanity.

[Christ Jesus] Who, being in very nature God, did not consider equality with God something to be used to his own advantage; rather, he made himself nothing by taking the very nature of a servant, being made in human likeness. And being found in appearance as a man, he humbled himself by becoming obedient to death—even death on a cross!

But, Paul's words also provide us with a challenge to emulate Christ's attitude and actions by, "not looking to your own interests, but each of you to the interests of the others" (Philippians 2:4). This has all the characteristics of servanthood, but expressed in tangible, lived action. It strikes at the heart of our identity, focusing on our intimate knowledge *of* Christ, which is born in relationship, rather than knowledge *about* Christ.

How to live in such a self-effacing manner in a self-oriented world can be puzzling. However, "how" questions often derail what is meant to be a servant-like *trust* issue. Questions such as "How is God present in Jesus Christ?", "How do we express faith in Jesus Christ?", and "How can Jesus be both human and divine?", are important and yet they can distract us into theoretical discussions that ultimately make no difference in our lives or in our world. In fact, many of these questions can be answered and still not lead to belief and to the consequent lifestyle of selflessness. The more important question is "who?"; "Who is Jesus?" And the answer is, he is God in the flesh; the God who loves his creation and desires to be near humanity, rather than just to fulfil a goal. If we have placed our trust in this God, then we must reflect his kind of ministry and leadership in our world. This means a commitment to stand with people no matter the circumstances and no matter the cost. We become the hands and feet of Jesus. In Jesus's own words:

> Then the righteous will answer him, "Lord, when did we see you hungry and feed you, or thirsty and give you something to drink? When did we see you a stranger and invite you in, or needing clothes and clothe you? When did we see you sick or in prison and go to visit you?" The king will reply, "Truly I tell you, whatever you did for one of the least of these brothers and sisters of mine, you did for me." (Matthew 25:37-40)

Care must be taken at this point. There is a fine line between living the calling and letting our ego get in the way. When this calling and ministry are so closely held to our identity and way of life, then criticism and opposition can feel like a direct assault on our personhood. We react badly, and often unpredictably, when this is the perception. It is even possible to rationalise away the criticism or opposition in spiritual terms and deceive ourselves into believing that we are on the moral high ground. This is countered when we understand, in ever-deepening measure, the new life we have in Christ. Ministry and leadership is not about us; it is about living as servants in the Kingdom of God! "We were therefore buried with him through baptism into death in order that, just as Christ was raised from the dead through the glory of the Father, we too may live a new life" (Romans 6:4).

Jesus is our model. Despite the agony of Gethsemane, when he prayed, "Father, if you are willing, take this cup from me" (Luke 22:42a), he continued to pray, "yet, not my will but yours be done" (Luke 22:42b). Wrapped up in living the calling to ministry and leadership is submission to God's agenda and his mission. In other words, we incarnate a trust relationship with Jesus Christ. Wesley wrote a prayer of commitment that captures this well.

> *I am no longer my own, but thine.*
> *Put me to what thou wilt, rank me with whom thou wilt.*
> *Put me to doing, put me to suffering.*
> *Let me be employed by thee or laid aside by thee.*
> *Exalted for thee or brought low for thee.*
> *Let me be full, let me be empty.*
> *Let me have all things, let me have nothing.*
> *I freely and heartily yield all things to thy pleasure and disposal.*[36]

All of life is an expression of our servanthood through incarnating a growing Christlikeness. The Apostle Paul, in speaking to his young protégé Timothy, outlines many characteristics of such a life: a leader is known for honesty, faithfulness in relationships, temperate, self-controlled, respectable, hospitable, moderate in use of drink and food, gentle, not argumentative, and has a wholesome family life where those closest to us respect us (see 1 Timothy 3:1-5). Notice that relationships are the priority. At its best, our spirituality is expressed through the quality of our relationships. "Anyone who claims to be in the light but hates a brother or sister is still in darkness. Anyone who loves their brother or sister lives in the light, and there is nothing in them to make them stumble" (1 John 2:9-10). Incarnating a deepening trust relationship with Christ shapes our other relationships and leads us onward toward Christlikeness.

Empowering Others as a Mandate for Ministry and Leadership

The idea of empowering others is implied in the previous emphases. If those in ministry and leadership are following God's agenda and incarnating Christ and his likeness through relationships, they are not the focus of attention. Instead, they redirect that focus by cooperating with God in what he is doing in his world. Although not easy, our task is simple; we are to reflect God's image (Christlikeness) and to make disciples. The reflecting of God's image is the *being* and the making of disciples is our *doing*.

It is interesting to note that in the Great Commission (Matthew 28:18-20) the main verb is *to make* (and the object is *disciples*). Some wrongly assume that *to go* shares the status of main verb. That is to say, *going* and *making disciples* are two separate, but equal actions; they are not. A better translation of *go* is, "in your going" or "while you are going." The assumption is that in your daily goings, you will make disciples. Furthermore, Jesus is not just speaking to pastors or leaders. All Christians are called to the task of making disciples while going about their various vocations. To emphasise the point once again, there are no professional disciple-makers. We are all called to be disciple-makers regardless of our vocations. Whether we are a teacher, tradesperson, labourer, sales person, student, driver, or even unemployed, we are to make disciples. This is the Great Commission. But, when do we know we have made a disciple? Based on this commission of Jesus, the answer is simple. Once someone we have been discipling is in turn discipling others, we have been successful in making a disciple.

Given that we all have the task of making disciples, the tasks of ministry and leadership are many and varied, depending upon context. Ephesians 4 emphasises at least two fundamental principles in the tasks of ministry. Firstly, despite a large variety of tasks, there is a unity in the purpose and fulfilment of these tasks. Paul uses the image of the "body" to describe the inherent unity of the ministry. "There is one body and one Spirit, just as you were called to one hope when you were called; one Lord, one faith, one baptism; one God and Father of all, who is over all and through all and in all" (Ephesians 4:4-6). There is a cohesiveness to this diversity that creates unity, not necessarily sameness. Common identity in Christ, common purpose, and common focus allow for this unique creation of unity. Peter uses the image of a building where all of us are "living stones" being built into one whole building, to become a holy priesthood (1 Peter 2:5). It is also interesting to note the plural pronouns in this verse; they imply community rather than individuality.

Secondly, Paul speaks of a diversity of gifts given "to equip his people [disciple-makers] for works of service [ministry], so that the Body of Christ may be built up until we all reach unity in the faith and in the knowledge of the Son of God" (Ephesians 4:12-13). In other words, we are to empower others for ministry and leadership. In this sense, a mature leader becomes the servant of the servants. This in no way absolves leaders from being disciple-makers and serving people. Many Christians have lost credibility within their own faith communities because they have failed to live out this disciple-making calling. Nevertheless, we do recognise that a calling to specific tasks requires specific gifting and abilities. God provides these gifts and abilities, and we are to use, cultivate, and develop them in service to others.

A word of warning. The multiplicity of giftedness and the equipping for service can quickly become institutionalised if we do not keep the major task of making disciples front and centre. Institutionalisation tends to be mostly negative. It creates: a rigid process that does not allow us to effectively change with a changing context (we get too comfortable with a certain way of doing things); a system that takes a lot of resource to keep going (think of all the committee meetings, phone calls, and emails necessary to keep a volunteer organisation running smoothly); a loss of focus on the main thing; and the development of transactional relationships rather than transformational ones.

Alan Hirsch speaks of what he terms the "Missional DNA" that is expressed in Ephesians 4.[37] While the term "missional" has become trendy and is often hard to define, Hirsch's descriptions of the gifts mentioned in Ephesians 4 are helpful. Although, remember, there is always the potential for distortion of these gifts as well. For example, *apostles* ensure that the faith is passed to other contexts and the next generation. People gifted in such a way think futuristically, thinking about establishing the church in new contexts and developing leadership to take the church where it is not yet. A downside is that unless other gifts are utilised, such as shepherding and teaching, people and organisations can feel used and simply a target to be reached.

The *prophets* are especially in tune with God and his communication for today. They challenge prevailing assumptions from our own contexts and question the *status quo*. There is an expectation by these people that all will heed God's call and obey. A limitation of those who work exclusively in this area of giftedness is that they often revel in the ideal and point to the imperfections of reality. As such they may be thought of as "other-worldly" and as having lost a sense of working with the world as it is.

The *evangelists* are those who recruit for the cause. They elicit a response to God's call in Christ and draw other believers into the wider mission, which is expressed in seeing the church grow. A drawback of those so gifted is that they can focus so much on reaching those outside the church that those within the church fail to get the attention needed to mature and be strengthened in their faith.

The *shepherds* nurture and protect those in the church. These gifted people focus on helping Christians mature in their faith. Shepherds cultivate a loving network of relationships as they seek to make disciples. This internal focus can lead to valuing stability to the detriment of mission outside of the church.

The *teachers* have the gift of understanding and explaining. They focus on remaining biblically grounded and guiding others in discerning God's will and way. They believe that helping people remain faithful to God's Word and knowing theological doctrines aids the maturing process and assist in focussing mission. However, without the other functions, teachers can fall into dogmatism or dry intellectualism.

Besides Ephesians 4, there are a number of other spiritual gifts lists given in Scripture, notably 1 Corinthians 12 and Romans 12; however, no two lists are identical (see Figure 2). This implies that these lists are more of a sample of what God gives us and are not exhaustive. Nevertheless, we will see some gifts more commonly expressed than others. Having an awareness of what the possibilities might be—and then

Romans 12	1 Corinthians	Ephesians 4	Other Passages
Exhortation	Administration	Apostle	Celibacy
Giving	Apostle	Evangelism	Hospitality
Leadership	Discernment	Pastor	Martyrdom
Mercy	Faith	Prophecy	Missionary
Prophecy	Healings	Teaching	Voluntary Poverty
Service	Helps		
Teaching	Knowledge		
	Miracles		
	Prophecy		
	Teaching		
	Tongues		
	Interpretation of Tongues		
	Wisdom		

Figure 2

prayerfully considering what our own giftedness might be—is an important part of a journey toward Christlikeness. We are created and fitted for a purpose.

One of the clear implication in our *doing* through these spiritual gifts, is that we are empowered by the Holy Spirit. While there is effort required on our part (training, education, planning, goal setting, monitoring, etc.), the element that makes us effective in what we do is God's empowerment. As leaders in ministry there is no place to boast on what may be achieved. We recognise that the achievement is the result of each of us working in our areas of giftedness. To be effective as leaders, then, we are required to release, encourage, and support others in their calling and areas of giftedness (cf. 1 Corinthians 3:5-9). A key question that we need to ask those coming into our congregation is, "How can we, as a faith fellowship, help you fulfil your calling in Christ?"

QUESTIONS FOR REFLECTION

1. Read Psalm 23. What are the key features of a "good shepherd" illustrated here. In what ways can you model the motif of "shepherd" in one or two of your ministry activities?

2. Read John 13:1-17 and reflect upon Jesus's servanthood attitude and actions. What might servanthood look like today in your context?

3. What are some of the pitfalls in a servanthood approach to ministry? How can these be avoided while still maintaining servanthood?

4. Why is incarnational ministry so important? What would incarnational ministry look like in your context?

5. How have you personally and your local church as a whole done at disciple-making? What needs to happen to make this more of a priority? How do you empower others to serve as part of your disciple-making?

CHAPTER 4

DOING OF MINISTRY AND LEADERSHIP

Thus far, the focus has been on *being* a reflector of God's image in us and on *being* empowered for service by God's Spirit. This is our created purpose and learning to *be* is a lifelong journey. The effective *doing* cannot take place without us *being* on the discipleship road of transformation toward Christlikeness. In this journey, God calls us to specific tasks of *doing*. Discerning this specific calling and the Spirit empowered giftedness that goes with this is the challenge for all involved in ministry and leadership.

Our Calling

Moses is a good, biblical example of one called by God to a specific task. God arrested Moses's attention through the burning bush in the desert and then proceeded to give him the task of leading God's people out of slavery in Egypt (Exodus 3–4). Moses was painfully aware of his inadequacies for this daunting task. As we read through the early life of Moses, we can see his passion for his people. However, we also see someone who tried to help and failed and someone who lacked the courage to follow through. Based on outward appearances and actions, Moses did not seem like the obvious or smart choice to lead the Children of Israel out of Egyptian slavery. However, God knew better. He knew who Moses was and knew who Moses could become. As Creator, God formed us with particular passions and talents and is calling us to embrace our purpose. As Ruth Haley Barton writes, "Vocation does not come from a voice 'out there' calling me to be something I am not. It comes from a voice 'in here' calling me to be the person I was born to be, to fulfil the original selfhood given to me at birth by God."[38]

Hindsight is a wonderful thing, and as we look back over Moses's life until his moment of calling, we can see how all his experiences contributed to shaping him into the person who could, with God's help, lead God's people out of slavery. He grew up in Pharaoh's court and knew the culture and political processes intimately. He had connections in the places of power. He was born a Hebrew and nurtured by his mother and family in the love of his birth people. He spent considerable time as a shepherd in the very desert through which he would lead God's people. Also, he had a clear passion for justice. All the raw material was there for God to shape and use for his purposes. Nevertheless, Moses still had to make a choice to embrace this calling and to trust God through this difficult journey.

The question with which we so often wrestle is our own specific calling. Many times, we can see God's hand at work in the life of someone else, but we find it difficult to translate that same perspective into our own life. So, the question is where to begin." We should begin with prayer asking God to reveal his calling to us. We should also assess our God-given talents and passions and explore how they might be used to fill a need in our community or in our world. Also, we should not be afraid to seek wise counsel from those who might know us better than we know ourselves. As we seek God's specific calling, we must remember that it comes to people in many different ways. Some receive a calling that is clear and exact, at a moment in time, that begins to transform their lives almost immediately. This was the case with my daughter BJ who responded to a call while she was "lost" at sea on a youth in mission trip to Fiji.[39] This experience shaped all subsequent life experiences and decisions for her. In my case, while I always had a sense of calling (maybe the result of growing up as the son of a pastor), the specifics of that call only emerged over time.[40] Whichever way we perceive the call, it is no less real or life transforming.

Doing God's Way

Having determined the specific call of God, we next realise that it usually requires us to "march to the beat of a different drum." Ministry and leadership in the Kingdom of God looks very different than service and leadership outside the Kingdom. Illustrative of this difference is the requirements that God imposed on Israel's choice of a would be future king. Moses outlined these as part of preparing the people of God for entry into the Promised Land.

The requirements were: (1) "Be sure to appoint over you a king the Lord your God chooses" (Deuteronomy 17:15). This was to be God's choice, so there was an implicit authority above that of the appointed king. (2) "The king, moreover, must not acquire great numbers of horses for himself or make the people return to Egypt to get more of them" (Deuteronomy 17:16). Horses were a symbol of military might and the king was not to rely upon military might to hold power. (3) "He must not take many wives, or his heart will be led astray" (Deuteronomy 17:17). Kings usually took foreign wives to help shore up their power; however, foreign wives usually brought in their own gods, which distracted Israel from the worship of Yahweh. The political alliances, often brokered through various marriages to neighbouring kingdoms, added a dimension of self-reliance rather than dependency on God. (4) "He must not accumulate large amounts of silver and gold" (Deuteronomy 17:17). Something of a foretaste of Jesus's words about how hard it was for a rich man to enter the Kingdom of God, Moses reminded the people that the king's authority was not to be found in such material possessions. Self-reliance for one's future has a selfish orientation that is not a reflection of trusting obedience in Yahweh. (5) "He is to write for himself on a scroll a copy of this law, taken from the Levitical priests. It is to be with him, and he is to read it all the days of his life so that he may learn to revere the Lord his God and follow carefully all the words of this law" (Deuteronomy 17:18,19). This king was to be one who took his instructions from God and his word. The king's authority was derived from his ongoing relationship with his God, not from some inherent positional title. Soaking in God's Word frequently was to be a reminder that God set the agenda, not the king. How different a king the king of Israel was to be from those of the neighbouring kingdoms!

These are important principles when it comes to thinking through the positioning of leadership and ministry activity in the Church. We are called of God (God's choosing), confirmed by the Church (recognised by appropriate character traits, giftedness and perhaps results), and empowered by the Holy Spirit. The confirmation of the Church in a formal way is often referred to as ordination. The Church of the Nazarene has checks and balances in its system to ensure quality candidates for ordination;[41] still, for the sake of the Church, due diligence must be taken by those charged with overseeing this process. Ordination candidates must recognise that ordination is not the end of the road for their preparation and development. While it is a significant accomplishment along the way, it is but a door to a whole journey of preparation, growing, further formal study, and intentional spiritual nurturement. Just as we are glad that our medical practitioners are required to keep up to date with medical research and the latest developments in health to keep their registration, how much more does a minister and leader in the Body of Christ need to keep current with the multitude of perspectives and developments in the areas of ministry, Bible, and theology and how these intersect with current issues in our world to be effective in our rapidly changing contexts.

Whether we be a lay person or an ordained minister, it is important to keep developing both our character and skills for ministry and leadership. Knowing where we are in a structure that nurtures growth and accountability is important. None of us can say that we have arrived at knowing all there is to know in ministry.

The Art of Theological Reflection

The practical implications of these principles are enormous. Christian ministry and leadership is all about what God is doing and how we might cooperate with him. One way we discern God's agenda and get on board with what he is doing is to learn the art of theological reflection. This is an intensely practical process that examines a specific experience through which we seek to learn about God's action. How does our faith inform our interpretation of God's action or how does the experience ask questions of our faith? This is the substance of theological reflection.[42]

Suppose a family you know well experiences an unexpected tragedy, such as a serious illness of the main income provider for that family. As you spend time with the family, including the sick member, lots of practical questions will emerge: "What is the prognosis for the sick member?"; "How do they ensure adequate health care?"; "What about the financial arrangements now?" Additionally, there will be other profound questions that arise as you work through the immediate crisis: "Where is God in this?"; "Why would God allow this to happen to us?"; "What do I tell my children?"; "What resources can I offer this family as they work through these deep questions?"; and many more! Questions begin to uncover theological assumptions we, or they, have made. These may have been unspoken and unquestioned for years. This is the fertile ground of theological reflection. So important a task is this, that it is doubtful that a person involved in ministry and leadership can survive very many years if they have not mastered this art.

In theological reflection, we begin by evaluating our experiences, including the everyday events in our lives. "Reflection as a method involves recognising what is in an event, naming it, relating it to other experiences and reflections, letting it shape the future."[43] This is a way of genuinely learning from and through our experiences. The good news is that we are not meant to tackle this alone. Firstly, we can rely upon the Holy Spirit to guide as we continue in prayerful conversation. Secondly, theological reflection is best conducted in a small group where those with differing perspectives to our own can contribute to our thinking. Still, none of this will help if we do not approach this with an open mind and spirit. Unfortunately, sometimes we can spend our time looking at experiences with a view to confirming what we already think we know or already believe. For the process of theological reflection to be genuinely transformational, we need to be open to hearing what is said. Often the greatest gift to be celebrated is becoming more receptive to the possibilities of this life as our worldviews are expanded and challenged by the diversity of people and perspectives.[44]

Different Perspectives on Leadership

There are many different ways that leadership is expressed in the church—all under the overarching theme of incarnational servanthood. This means that the *doing* in ministry may look differently from place to place and person to person. However, it is helpful to apply the lens of biblical principles and theological coherence to the varied leadership approaches to ensure appropriateness for the church. One way of understanding the differences is to think in terms of a continuum between focusing on the leader and focusing on the people. The context in which leadership is conducted will also influence the expression of leadership. Consider the continuum like this:

Leader Focused - - - - - Context - - - - - People Led

For example, *trait leadership* is an approach that focusses almost exclusively on the leader. Certain traits or innate talents are suggested as vital for leadership. Unfortunately, there is no real consensus on what these traits ought to be. Such things as ambition, energy, desire to lead, honesty, integrity, self-confidence, intelligence, and job-relevant knowledge are identified, but are leaders simply born with these talents? Many would answer yes, also noting the need for cultivation. Similarly, *skill leadership* focuses more intently on the leader's technical, human, and conceptual skills. There is room in this perspective to understand that skills may be developed. In a slight shift in focus away from the leader, *behavioural* or *style leadership* examines the personality of the leader and whether the leader has a predisposition toward people or tasks. There are many additional examples of leadership approaches;[45] the point is, many of these perspectives can legitimately express the biblical principles of incarnation and servant leadership. Thus, the *doing* of ministry is diverse and will look differently.

Arguably one of the most popular approaches used in recent years within church circles has been the *transformational leadership* approach.

Its popularity is found in its congruence with incarnational and servant-hood leadership principles of Scripture. As with any of these approaches, it can be used in a non-biblical way. However, at its best, this approach is very useful. Transformational leadership does not lend itself to a simple, single sentence definition, but the primary idea is that the leader is a catalyst for a process that transforms people rather than simply guiding them to a particular goal. The transformation is potentially profound as it involves emotions, values, ethics, standards, and long-term goals of the individuals involved. The focus is upon those being led and their needs to flourish as authentic persons. Such transformation leads people in a group or community to accomplish more than is usually expected of them through an exceptional form of influence. Both the leader and the people being led are bound together in the transformational process so that all are changed for the better.

Transformational leadership is sometimes referred to as *value-added* leadership because the key to moving followers to extraordinary performance is the adding of values that change their world view and internally motivate people to do and be more than expected. For example, adopting the values of loving others, self-sacrifice, servanthood, which are often referred to as "Kingdom values," will change us and our ministry. The counter-point to *transformational* leadership is *transactional* leadership which typically involves contracts, expectations, and job descriptions. These are constructed to meet specific guidelines and in one sense sets the "ceiling" of expectations and results. There is a place for transactional leadership since activities need to be done in an orderly and predictable fashion. Indeed, legal requirements often require a significant contractual approach when working with people and organisations such as churches. Often there will be an interplay between transactional and transformational approaches. Transactional leadership can be thought of in terms of management, while transformational leadership can be considered the major domain of leadership. Figure 3 gives a simple comparison between the two.[46] While this comparison is somewhat simplistic, it does illustrate that a different mix of gifts is required for each of these two approaches. One is not right and the other wrong, but each has an appropriate place in ministry that needs to be affirmed by those with other gift orientations.

An approach that focusses on people, intentionally cultivating values that will transform lives, and is both respectful of the individual, as well as the group, is very attractive from a Biblical standpoint. This, of course, is the ultimate lens through which we, in ministry and Christian leadership want to view our actions. Because of the focus on relationships, the transformational leadership approach is sometimes termed *relational leadership*. Figure 4 gives a comparison between the two perspectives.[47]

SUBJECT	MANAGER	LEADER
Make up of role	Stability	Change
Decision making	Makes	Facilitates
Approach	Plans details around constraints	Sets and leads direction
Vision	Short-term: today	Long-term: Horizon
Control	Formal Influence	Personal charm
Appeals to	The head	The heart
Culture	Endorses	Shapes
Action	Reactive	Proactive
Risk	Minimises	Takes
Rules	Makes	Breaks
Direction	Existing direction / keeps the status quo	New directin / challenges the norm
Values	Results	Achievement
Concern	Doing the thing right	Doing the right thing
Focus	Managing work	Leading people
Human Resources	Subordinates	Followers

Figure 3

As people are increasingly transformed by these values and adopt, there is an interesting shift away from a reliance on institutionalised and positional authority to one that is internally driven. Thomas Sergiovanni describes the different sources of authority as:

1. Traditional (positional and institutional) authority expects people to follow because of the position in the system held by the leader.

2. Psychological authority emphasises the motivational aspects of self-interest of the follower.

Transactional Leader	Relational (Transformational) Leader
Exchange what they do for what you can do for them	Prefer to give more than they receive
Measures success or failure by metrics	See success in transformed individuals and social systems
Motivate with rewards and punishments	Motivate with higher ideals and moral values
Set goals	Help followers set their own goals
Cast vision	Create a shared vision
View followers as subordinates	Engage followers as partners in a common mission
Put welfare of organisation first	Put welfare of people first
In business, want to make a sale	In business, want to keep customers coming back
Ends justify the means – whatever works	Means are primary – whatever is right
Seek benefits and bonuses	Serve causes greater than themselves

Figure 4

3. Technical-rational authority expects the followers to follow what is considered true.

4. Professional authority is based upon the seasoned craft knowledge and personal expertise of the leader.

5. Moral authority highlights the obligation derived from widely shared values, ideas and ideals.[48]

It is into this fifth area of authority that transformational leadership moves. People who are driven by a sense of moral authority, internally driven from shared values, will ultimately achieve far beyond expectations. The confines of a transactional approach are removed and people are freed from limiting expectations. Personal and group transformation will be the consequence. Moral authority is clearly one of the strongest forms of authority, for it is not externally imposed. Nevertheless, for moral leadership to genuinely be the guide, people need to be released and trusted so that they can be governed by this moral authority. Since personal and community values are crucial to the *doing* of transformational leadership, we must know and understand the values of the Kingdom of God. It is to this we now turn our attention.

Kingdom Values

Jesus's Sermon on the Mount (Matthew 5–7) is a great summary of Kingdom values, which are often counter-intuitive and counter-cultural. The Beatitudes at the beginning of the sermon (Matthew 5:3-12) establish the attitudes that become values out of which we act (the "*be*-attitudes," as it were). These are not statements but exclamations of affirmation.[49]

"Blessed are the poor in spirit, for theirs is the kingdom of heaven" (Matthew 5:3). The paucity of spirit affirmed here is the humility to recognise that we come to God with nothing to offer but ourselves. Rather than come to ministry with the idea that we have plenty to contribute, we come simply offering ourselves for God to use. Our confidence comes from our dependency upon God, rather than in our own abilities. This helps the minister to listen well and to seek God's agenda.

"Blessed are those who mourn, for they will be comforted" (Matthew 5:4). The value of the broken heart may appear very counter-intuitive, but this is what Jesus is saying. Hope is found even within the desperately painful moments of loss. In those moments when it appears that all is lost, God does bring comfort. He does care and embrace us at the point of our need. Ministry and leadership include responding with compassion and hope in dire circumstances. There is an optimism that breaks through the clouds of despair and pain. It is a hope-filled approach to ministry and leadership that is not destroyed by difficulty and despair. For example, Moses could respond to God's call to bring the Children of Israel out of slavery and despair and into the Promised Land—the optimism of God's comfort!

"Blessed are the meek, for they will inherit the earth" (Matthew 5:5). The value of meekness is a balanced self that knows the limits of its own resources and an openness to learn and receive. This teachable spirit has the strength to be angry at the right time, self-controlled and humble.[50] People involved in ministry and leadership should not be arrogant or self-serving. Perhaps *The Message* paraphrase captures this value best—"You're blessed when you're content with just who you are—no more, no less. That's the moment you find yourselves the proud owners of everything that can't be bought" (Matthew 5:5).

"Blessed are those who hunger and thirst for righteousness, for they will be filled" (Matthew 5:6). What we ultimately pursue in life will shape our personhood, ministry, and leadership.[51] There is no place for shallow, self-oriented motivations in ministry. Otherwise, we will be forever looking for "greener pastures," or develop a drivenness that will be destructive. Pursuing God's righteousness is the most fulfilling journey we can take. This is because we are being shaped God's creative purpose and agenda. We work hard but relax in the reality that God has designed us for such a journey. We are fit for purpose! Ministry and leadership become sustainable as a result.

"Blessed are the merciful, for they will be shown mercy" (Matthew 5:7). The value of mercy, as expressed by Jesus, is more than a sympathy and a softness of heart. There is firstly a recognition that we are the recipient of God's mercy ourselves, and we can do no less than respond in mercy to others. Secondly, those who have mercy deeply identify with those who need mercy—to journey with someone in their desperate need. As we walk alongside someone who has reached the end of their own resources, our lives echo Christ's incarnational approach to ministry. A generosity of spirit, an acceptance of the other, and an acknowledgement of the fact that "there but for the grace of God go I" that is reflected in the actions of ministry.

"Blessed are the pure in heart, for they will see God" (Matthew 5:8). The value of authenticity and purity of intention is encompassed here. While many may start serving others for less than pure intentions (such as satisfying the need to be needed, the need for control, the need to be well thought of by others, etc.) the demands of ministry and leadership require a regular, disciplined self-examination to recognise and remove that which is impure. This is a demanding and sometimes a costly exercise for all of us.

"Blessed are the peacemakers, for they will be called children of God" (Matthew 5:9). Peacemaking is a challenging. The term *peace* is more than the absence of conflict. It involves wholeness, health, balance, and reconciled relationships. As this relates to ministry and leadership, we see God's agenda—the reconciliation of people to God and each other. In our world of fractured relationships, selfishness, and domination, we are to value peaceful reconciliation. Ministry is not meant to polarise and draw lines in the sand, but rather to develop places of grace, mercy, forgiveness and reconciliation. If peacemaking is a genuine value, then these will be features of ministry.

"Blessed are those who are persecuted because of righteousness, for theirs is the kingdom of heaven" (Matthew 5:10). It is interesting that in spite of passionately pursing righteousness and seeking to bring God's peace, Jesus anticipated persecution because of these actions. The value expressed here is, by implication, courage and resiliency. Doing ministry is for the long haul. It is not a brief season of fun and then a move to something different. Like Abraham, when needing to decide with nephew Lot to take the easy well-watered plains for his stock or take the hard, rugged hills as his portion of land (see Genesis 13:8-13), we are sometimes called to take the hard, less popular road for sake of ministry. Ministry and leadership look more like a marathon than a hundred-metre sprint.

In summary, the values of the Kingdom of God, counter-intuitive as they may be, will shape what our ministry and leadership will look like. There is something distinctive to ministry as we adopt the Kingdom values of humility, brokenness, righteousness, mercy, authenticity, peacemaking, resiliency, and courage. I pray that God will help us to live in his Kingdom in such a way that we will genuinely be light in very dark places and salt in areas of blandness. There is spice and vitality to ministry and leadership as we increasingly reflect these values.

QUESTIONS FOR REFLECTION

1. What do you discern as your gifts in ministry? What is your calling and how do these gifts contribute to that calling? How will you intentionally cultivate these gifts?

2. How do you translate the emphasis of Deuteronomy 17:15-19 into doing your ministry God's way?

3. Read the following account of a church situation and reflect upon the provide questions.

> B and D have two children, a toddler and a pre-schooler. They attend church most Sundays for the past two years. They have developing relationships with some members of the congregation. While B (wife and mother) has grown up in a church of a similar tradition, D (husband and father) has only been around church since being married to D. He appears to take seriously being a good father and husband, so he "tags along" with B when she attends church. However, he appears not to know much about the Christian faith of how church life functions. There are very few other children in the congregation, but B enjoys the motherly relationships with several of the older women in the church. The children are too young for the children's church and Sunday School that is provided.

Just recently T, one of the matriarchs of the church, had words with B about the behaviour of her children. T was troubled at the noise of the children during the service and the fact that they were "constantly moving around the building and causing a distraction". B and D were upset by this encounter and are now considering whether they should find another more receptive congregation for their young family to worship.

As a member of the pastoral care team in the congregation you have observed the growing tension between T, B and D. What do you do in this situation? Why?

   a. What is happening in this encounter?

   b. Are there particular understandings of God revealed in this?

   c. What is God doing here?

   d. What theological themes are present in this encounter? E.g. God's love, redemption, forgiveness/lack of forgiveness, etc.

   e. What would you do next in this encounter and why?

4. Which of the different leadership perspectives do you encounter in your own context? In what ways do those in leadership positions around you reveal these perspectives? What is your own style? What do you see as the strengths and weakness of your own style?

5. How might transformational leadership perspectives be included in your ministry activity? What is the weighting of *transactional* compared to *transformational* leadership activity expressed in your current ministry setting? Give evidence of the weighting. How do you relate to the committee or board and to those immediately above you in leadership?

CHAPTER 5

INCARNATING MINISTRY AND LEADERSHIP

On this journey, we have explored the *being* of discipleship and the focus on character development and spiritual formation as essential for involvement in effective Christian ministry and leadership. The Biblical base has provided a scaffold upon which to build a concept of ministry and leadership compatible with Kingdom of God principles. Many of these values are counter-intuitive, and we need to intentionality incorporate them into our lives. Values and transformative elements of discipleship are to be lived out. This is not a theoretical discussion to continue a routine that does not deepen our relationship with God and others. The ultimate challenge of ministry and leadership is to bring together *being* and *doing* in such a way that the *doing* is an expression of who we are, not simply an expression of a job description. This is living incarnationally.

A People Focus

As the Apostle Paul teaches us, truth is embodied, and people become the testimony to our effectiveness in ministry and leadership.

> Are we beginning to commend ourselves again? Or do we need, like some people, letters of recommendation to you or from you? You yourselves are our letter, written on our hearts, known and read by everyone. You show that you are a letter, written on our hearts, known and read by everyone. You show that you are a letter from Christ, the result of our ministry, written not with ink but with the Spirit of the living God, not on tablets of stone but on tablets

> of human hearts. Such confidence we have through Christ before God. Not that we are competent in ourselves to claim anything for ourselves, but our competence comes from God. He has made us competent as ministers of a new covenant - not of the letter but of the Spirit; for the letter kills, but the Spirit gives life. (2 Corinthians 3:1-6)

Therefore, the immediate implication for incarnational ministry and leadership is that people and relationships are the primary focus. The development of community is essential. In many societies, there is little emphasis or time spent in developing true community. For example, in Australia, generations ago the family formed the basis for this community; however, families look very different today. According to the latest Australian census, there are six million families (in a population of twenty-five million), 45% couples with children, 38% couples with no children, 24% living in single person households, and almost 0.1% same sex couples.[52] Cultivating positive relationships will take intentionality in this new reality.

Some have highlighted the potentially detrimental role of technology in communication as a contributing factor in this new reality. The accessibility of communication technology has led to the prioritising of *timeliness* in communication, over the role of *space* in communication. This shift feeds into an already troubling trend of failing relational connections between people. Even when we are physically present and in conversation with each other, we often allow the interruption of the text message or phone call to take priority. *Hospitable presence*[53] is minimised or unwittingly devalued because of the interruption. Ironically, in an age that values connection, it is the detached connection of technology that appears to take precedence over physical presence and immediate communication. Just as troubling is the meta-message that is communicated as a result. Preferring the one interrupting over the one physically present can communicate that the person remote to the scene is of more importance. This often feeds into a narcissism that is not only destructive in the communication process, but does not reflect well biblical values.[54]

To bow to this often-subversive process is to trend to the consumeristic, individualism that is rampant in many cultures today.

This is not just an issue for home life; we must seriously consider how we communicate within the church. Do we cultivate a hospitable presence that allows for genuine community to develop? Are we continually distracted with competing communicative demands? What meta-message is the short attention span and interruptions communicating to the community of faith? The challenge of living incarnationally and relationally is to cultivate a hospitable presence and an availability to the other person. Even as we contemplate the best way to reach the next generation, we must recognise that technology and programs can never replace relationships.

There is a place for technology, but the effective management of its use is the challenge for every leader. Gregory Spencer gives five practical steps to aid an incarnational coming alongside people in such a technological context. He says, firstly, to make life affirming decisions about time and space. Secondly, choose the best method to accomplish the task. *Facebook* has a place, but the form needs to match the message. Thirdly, try and use as many senses as possible in the communicative process—not just words, but our bodies and their senses. Fourthly, recognise that meta-messages do matter and this message ought to be that we give our undivided attention to those with whom we are communicating at that moment. Fifthly, make relational choices with a view to the long term. Do not look for the quick fix, which is often superficial.[55]

Two important elements to this relational approach to ministry and leadership come to mind. Firstly, we must learn the art of *walking slowly with others*.[56] My daughter BJ epitomized *walking slowly with others* in her missionary career in Thailand. Those that worked closely with her speak of the way she put other people first: she opened her home to the many children and adults so that they could be part of more than just her work life; she was patient with people's shortcomings; she expressed her love through action and by spending time with people; she made room in her schedule for people who would serendipitously come across her way; and she learned to be flexible in a culture very different from her own.[57] This is an apt description of relational ministry.

When we feel passionate about being part of the Kingdom of God and seeking every opportunity to disciple people along the way, we can become impatient at the slowness of the journey. The larger narrative that gets communicated in this impatience is that we have a personal (self-serving) agenda. We must cultivate a *slow church*[58] mentality. If we are in such a rush to see increased numbers, to improve efficiency, and to control the unpredictable nature of relationships, then, we are not serious about incarnational ministry. We must be more intentional about rooting ourselves into a community and finding avenues to live out the love of Christ in ways to which those around us can relate.

The second element to this relational approach is an open-ended commitment to living our lives with people. The sacrificial giving of time is crucial here. While relationships are primary, people are not just a "target" for evangelism. They are important for who they are already. In living out the values of the Kingdom, the claims of the Gospel are expressed through relationships and time spent together. There is a dynamic sense in which making disciples and seeing people grow in their reflection of God's image is a natural consequence of living incarnationally. Serving people has a way of spreading love that transforms. Practically speaking, this open-ended commitment is time consuming. We cannot be in a rush. Gentle intentionality is the process to use.

Strategies and Goals

Incarnational ministry and leadership focuses on people, but it should not lead us to believe there is no need for setting goals and planning strategies. These are important aspects of our accountability to and communication with the Body of Christ. It is important to understand that these goals and strategies are developed in the context of community and in living incarnationally. Yes, our priorities need to be realigned with Kingdom values, and there needs to be acknowledgement of God's priorities. Still, this realignment can lead to God-glorifying goals and strategies.

A question that is often asked is, "Who sets the vision for a local church from which goals and strategies are developed?" This is usually asked when there is a difference of opinion about the vision. Context and circumstance are important as we try to answer this significant question. With a new church plant, it is often the leader who interprets what God is doing in the community and then invites people to commit to this vision. He or she often gathers like-minded people to form a team. However, in the case of an existing congregation, with a substantial history of ministry, the vision is much more likely to be developed as a shared task. This process is usually more complex since there needs to be significant time and space for conversation, listening to one another, and discerning together what God is saying to the congregation. The leader, while instrumental in this process, is not necessarily the one to set the vision. It is developed from within the body of believers. This takes a different kind of leadership approach to that of the church planter.

A leader in an existing congregation should encourage members to engage people outside of the church in conversation to hear the heartbeat of the community. As the members of the faith community gather for prayer and reflection on what they have heard in the community, they should consider the following: "What is our passion? What burns on our hearts? Why are we here?"[59] This will no doubt take numerous conversations. However, as the congregation prayerfully considers the needs of the community in light of the mission of God, a sense of calling will emerge that the congregation will understood as *their* calling. In essence, they will begin to see what God is already doing in their community and cooperate with God in his activity. This journey is neither for the fainthearted nor the impatient!

Let us return to the issue of goals and strategies with an emphasis on *being*. We might think that developing goals and strategies for ministry are at best irrelevant or at worst a distraction that reeks of a focus on human effort. Nothing could be further from the truth! If we keep a strong grounding in who we are as growing disciple of Christ (our *being*), our human activity will be guided by the Holy Spirit in a way that is

Christocentric. Goals in ministry and leadership are needed for at least the following reasons:

1. Goals are an expression of what we understand is important.[60] Values are expressed in what we aim for. For example, if we value reaching people for Christ and spend the vast majority of our money and time on renovating or looking after a building, then our actions and words don't match. Goals help us keep the focus right.

2. Goals can be stepping stones along the way to a larger strategy to fulfil a vision that we have discerned as God's calling. While visions are usually much larger enterprises, having smaller measurable goals along the way will keep us encouraged.

3. Goals are a way for us to articulate exactly what it is we are trying to achieve with God's help. Sometimes we can have difficulty being practical enough to identify a way forward, but goals help to give particularity and clarity to our activities. A stated goal might be to involve twenty percent of our congregation in community services outside the church (e.g. Parent & Community Committee at a local school, chaplaincy committee, foodbank, domestic violence shelter, young mothers club, motor cycle club, sports club ... the list can go on!). Such a goal would be just the first step of mobilisation, but it is specific and measurable. Another significant conversation to have would be on how the friends made in these circles can then be impacted by our faith fellowship.

4. Goals can be a means to hold us accountable for ministry activities.[61] This is not intended to highlight our failures. Goals are meant to be points for celebration when achieved or points of clarification to review the strategy when we fall short. In the spirit of being held accountable for our personal journey of faith through a mentor or discipler, so too, are we are to be held accountable for group processes. At no point do we lay blame when we fail to attain our goal. Rather the language of "we" is used to recommit and to refocus on

doing better next time. This language shift from "you" to "we" is important in developing a culture that is mutually supportive and mutually accountable.

5. Goals help measure what matters. To hold each other accountable and to be able to celebrate the successes, we need to make sure that we measure what matters.[62] Trivial goals or awards tend to lessen the value of the overall task. There is often debate about counting the number of people in church on a Sunday or at a particular event. Some would prefer to talk about "just being faithful" and ignore whether the tasks are effective or not. Measuring is important if we know why we are counting a particular statistic. The reasons to the "why" and the "what" need to be wholesome, God-glorifying reasons and results that reflect our calling and values.

6. Goals help us check on *mission drift*.[63] Without a regular review on progress toward our goals we may find that we have been involved in activities, while good in and of themselves, that have not adequately reflected the values we feel called to reflect. Carrying on this way, we may never reach the goals we have intended.

Administration

Being involved in the leadership of a congregation involves administration. This is the planning, reporting, record keeping, rostering, communicating, book keeping, etc. that is associated with ministry activity. Subtly, administrative tasks can take over most of the energy of a group. Before long the goals can become focused on internal activities that are designed to prop up the "machinery" of the church while the mission is relegated to the less important. Just as importantly, a person can be so caught up with a calling to reach people for Christ that they leave administration undone or done poorly. Obviously, a balance is required. This balance can be brought about by each member mutually respecting the contribution of the other toward the shared vision. One emphasis is not right and the other wrong. The administration is often understood in management terms rather than leadership terms. Both are needed!

A practical way of looking at the Body of Christ is as a team. The exploration of how teams function well and what happens when things go wrong has developed over several years in both the Christian and secular environments.[64] While much of this is intuitive, care must be taken to apply a team perspective in the conduct of ministry and leadership. Collaborative working and decision-making are key features of this process. Becoming a healthy team will enhance ministry and leadership. A healthy team will trust each other, empower each other, assimilate (incorporate new people in the team to work alongside us), manage well, and serve.[65] They will also have clear, elevating goals, a results-driven structure, competent team members, unified commitment, a collaborative environment, standards of excellence, external support and recognition, and principled leadership.[66]

As a team player, it is important to know your place in the team. What is it that you contribute to the overall team and ministry? What gifts do you bring to this team that complement the gifts of others? If you can develop a team yourself, make sure that you find members who are different from you. It is easier to work with people like yourself, but this does not make for a strong team. Seek out people who will complement (not compliment!) your strengths. StrengthsFinders[67] is one program that can help you determine your strengths and those of your team. This diversity will make it more difficult to keep connected and working together, so one of the key features essential in a team player is humility. That is, being open to hearing what others of the team are saying, even when we disagree or struggle to understand each other's perspective.[68]

In ministry and leadership, we will be a part of several teams. The whole congregation can be understood as a team, just as easily as a church board or ministry group. One of the implications of being a team member is knowing when to involve other more qualified persons. One should not presume to be able to address all issues that come your way, either in a pastoral sense or in an administrative area. Key questions such as, "Who else should know about this?", "Do I have the authority or responsibility to address this myself?", "Do I have the expertise necessary to address this?", need to be considered before acting or making a decision.

Work on committees and boards are an important part of leadership. It is there that the quality of the ministry rises or falls. It is not just about the administration, but rather the way issues are approached and decisions made. As a member of a committee or aboard, you have the responsibility of being transparent and courageous enough to share your opinions and ideas. However, there will be times when the decision of the meeting will not go the way you would prefer it to go. Once the decision is made, you must be a promoter of that decision as much as the person who advocated for the idea. Communication, both within the committee and outside, is to be positive and united. The assumption is, of course, that the decision-making process allowed for good expression of views and that a generous spirit prevailed. Should this not be the case, then poor decisions will result. Tensions will arise that have the potential of derailing ministry and leadership. The chair of the meeting has the responsibility to ensure that everyone is heard respectfully.

In small teams and committees, it is important to aim for consensus. If the decision is decided by close vote, then more time is needed (not necessarily at the same meeting) to process all that has happened. There is a temptation to refer to *Robert's Rules of Order* and push the decision through. The role of such rules is to ensure balance and fairness in discussion, usually in larger meetings. If the rules are used to stifle discussion or to confuse, then inevitably, this will lead to polarisation. While someone may prevail on the issue using such a process, the larger ministry ethos is lost and trust is eroded. Key questions to consider are: Has everyone been heard? Has everyone been treated with respect? Are relationships restored? Is everyone who needs to be at the discussion, present? The temptation is to lose patience with the process. Occasionally there will be one or two members who will be less than helpful in their contributions and the issue at hand is derailed once more. If this continues, the issue tends to be something other than the presenting issue. Perhaps the interference is the result of poor relationships, the inability to think as part of a team, or a personal aversion to risk-taking. Settle the main issue and come back to the presenting issue later. It is possible to agree to disagree and continue in a positive, loving relationship. That is the Gospel at work!

Conflict Resolution

Where there is a diversity of people, there will be conflict; it is inevitable. Well intentioned people will clash with each other. The presence of conflict is not bad, but the way it is addressed may be healthy or unhealthy. Effective teams know how to manage conflict well. Houston Thompson offers us wise words when he writes:

> Many times, conflict provides a framework for seeing a situation through a different lens. We may have looked at a program, a ministry, or a person one way for years. Then something happens that forces us to think, see, or act differently. When this occurs, we have a choice. We can call this difference conflict, or we can embrace the difference as an opportunity. It really is a matter of perspective.[69]

It must be remembered that we usually work with volunteers in noncontractual associations. Lines of authority are not always clear, and it is not always possible to demand a response. Choosing the method of addressing conflict will take wisdom. Becoming a person or organisation that is confident dealing with conflict, strengthens ministry and leadership.[70] Thompson's "Six C's model" is an example of options that could be considered when facing conflict.[71] Becoming familiar with options such as these can provide a more measured and balanced approach to conflict resolution.

There are two aspects that need to be clearly understood as we seek to resolve conflict. Firstly, a recognition of the *interdependence* between the parties or people that has created the conflict in the first place. If there was no sense of interdependence there would be no motive or desire to seek a resolution. This is positive as it shows a degree of care about the issue. It is on this element of care that we can potentially build a platform for resolution. Secondly, the *perception* of the conflict can vary greatly and is complex in nature. The perception of conflict can be real or imagined but finds itself in what we *think* we know.[72] Grappling with the variations of what we each think we know about the conflict is an important step toward deciding the way to resolve it.

Once we have a deeper understanding of the conflict, we can begin to reframe it in a way that can lead toward positive outcomes. Compare some reframing possibilities reflected in a simple choice of words (see Figure 5).[73]

Positive Approach	Negative Approach Difficult
Interaction	Contest
Mutual Benefit	Win or Lose
Interdependence	Control
Opportunity	Problem
Difference	Dispute
Exchange	Struggle
Persuade	Manipulate
Exciting	Frightening
Stimulating	Tension
Challenging	Difficult

Figure 5

While conflict is never easy, it does provide the opportunity for growth, both for the Christian and the community of faith. Developing effective strategies for working with conflict creates a healthy environment in which to conduct ministry and leadership. Four approaches that can help, regardless of the ultimate strategy used for resolution, are: (1) delay responding to the conflict while emotions are running high; (2) think reflectively once away from the heat of the moment; (3) listen for understanding and perspective; and (4) allow for honest and straightforward communication.[74] This can only be built on trust.

Pastoral Care

One major area of ministry, that has suffered from a lack of focus in recent times, is that of pastoral care. Some would rather do pastoral care without the face-to-face encounter that is so important in using all the senses of communication for understanding. Generally, emails, texts, and *Facebook* are poor substitutes for that face-to-face pastoral encounter. When this kind of technology becomes the communication standard, then incarnational ministry is lost. Some may argue that this is a better way of reaching more people. Of course, it is less messy to work with texts and emails, but there is also less engagement. The question is always, "What is the larger message being delivered when we use processes that avoid or minimise personal encounter?"

Pastoral care is not just about responding to crises and people's needs. There is a proactive element to pastoral care that is important to address. Some ways this can be done include:

1. Providing opportunity to fellowship around a meal. Tea before and after church gatherings also provides opportunity for connection as well as opportunity for people to use their ministry gift of hospitality. A word of caution here. People using their gifts in hospitality need to be affirmed, but they also need to be aware of why they are doing their activity, such as providing the morning tea. They are providing hospitality space. Sometimes well-meaning people want to dictate the process for efficiency, but create tension as a result. This does not help provide a gentle relational space for proactive pastoral care. Seemingly small things are very important in proactive pastoral care. Some of your most important people are those with the gift of hospitality.

2. Developing a shared ministry experience that draws people together around a common focus. They learn, laugh, pray, and grow together as a result. A regular feature of one youth group was a mission trip overseas. The group would meet weekly for six months prior to the trip. They would pray, prepare, and follow the same daily Bible readings for the six months. Many of those young people

became strong Christians. Involvement in a Work & Witness team can have similar results. I remember one member of a congregation who had been a loyal, but somewhat negative influence within the congregation, until he went on a Work & Witness team trip. His testimony on his return was that for the first time in his life he felt God had used him in tangible ways. It seems that his years of negativity was the result of not knowing how to involve himself in ministry.

3. Implement a systematic way that every member of the congregation is visited at a convenient location outside of the regular church activities. Showing we care opens the door to a deeper relationship. The process needs to be systematic so that no one is excluded. Making contact outside of the regular church activity times shows we value the person. This kind of contact can be quite a challenge within the busyness of life and the frenetic pace lived by so many.

4. Developing a network of communication to hear of important events in the life of members of the congregation. Involvement in people's lives and sharing together the events that can be celebrated, prayed for, or simply noted in a care-filled way.

5. Never do a ministry activity alone. Mentor someone as part of the process! Ministry is not just what we do on Sunday; therefore, we must ensure that there are the hospital visits, the home visits, the attendance at the sports event, or celebrating with those graduating. It is a matter of "doing life" together.

Proactive pastoral care is a fun-filled part of ministry. It is an incredible privilege to be a part of people's lives. Nevertheless, there are times when crises come. When involved in pastoral care, we may have the privilege of journeying with people through difficult and often messy times. One of the greatest gifts we can give someone in crisis is a non-judgemental, caring presence. Often people are unsure of what to say in moments of crisis, but words are usually not needed.

In my own journey through the loss of my daughter to cancer there were a couple of practical things that were (or I wish were) done that helped. Firstly, the physical presence of one or two caring individuals who did not stay long but took the time to drop in and express love and support. Secondly, the occasional prayer or reading of a passage of Scripture to bring light in our darkness was deeply appreciated. A couple of people from a neighbouring church gave practical support by way of meals for several days after my daughter's passing. Thirdly, providing opportunities to talk about our loved one who is no longer with us. Times of reflection and conversation helped us begin to deal with the deep void. We needed to process that verbally as difficult as this was to do. Fourthly, remembering various "firsts" was important to us: the first Christmas without her, her birthday, the first Mother's Day and Father's Day without her, etc. For someone to remember the pain that we were experiencing on one of those "firsts" days was a comfort.

These suggested pastoral activities are small in and of themselves, but they have a profound impact. This is part of "doing life" with people and being attentive to their experiences. In many respects, when someone visits because that is their job—it is expected. When someone visits because they care—that has impact! Pastoral care is time consuming, and yet, this is real life. Being "busy" and doing "what is important" are not necessarily the same thing. We need to develop the capacity "to be unhurried with another person."[75] As I reflect on my daughter's incredibly busy life, even while struggling with cancer, she always had time for people. When friends would come by to see her, often unexpectedly, time spent with them felt like the most important time of her day. Her friends left feeling like my daughter had waited for that very moment for their visit. *Hospitable presence* is an amazing gift that those of us who are involved in pastoral care can cultivate.

Pastoral care is an area where we need to know our personal limits. Well intentioned actions on our part can turn horribly wrong if we do not abide by a few simple, common sense guidelines. Firstly, we are not qualified counsellors. Most of us do not have any training in this field, and if we are not careful, we have gleaned just enough to be dangerous.

Many people will come to us with issues that have deep seated roots. Our role as caregivers is to walk with people who need counselling as they seek more intensive and professional help. We are their companion on the journey, not the one to diagnose and treat. Always ask yourself, "Is this a situation where I need to refer this person to a professional? Can this person benefit from the input of a professional?" When in doubt, refer! One of the greatest resources with which you can provide the faith community is a list of well-respected professional practitioners in such fields as psychology, medicine, social work, and justice. On occasion, it is the caring and trusting relationship of a lay pastor that gives a person the courage to seek professional help.

Secondly, our personal integrity is under scrutiny. We must always act ethically and appropriately. Often, we are working with vulnerable people, and we need to be sensitive to the potential that others may attempt to manipulate us or foster an unhealthy dependency upon us. The people for whom we care are responsible for their actions and decisions, and they should be guided to accept that responsibility. Therefore, our engagement with others must reflect respect for their personhood. This includes having appropriate boundaries when dealing with people of both sexes. It is easy to develop inappropriate relationships with those in need, so we must know the limits of healthy intrusiveness. Confidentiality plays a key part in the cultivation of a culture of trust and respect, as does a sense of love and care. The words we use, the kind of humour we engage in, and the responses to what is often the ugly side of life will make or break us as pastoral caregivers. A healthy dose of humility flowing from a heart filled with love for Jesus Christ and others will help us in this vital area of Christian ministry and leadership.

QUESTIONS FOR REFLECTION

1. Think about the way in which you use technology and social media in your life and ministry. What aspects need improvement? Make a plan to address these areas. How might you cultivate "hospitable presence" in your ministry?

2. Express a vision for the ministry in which you are involved. Where did this vision come from—you, a Board, a group of like-minded people, after a period of discernment?

3. List a series of goals that reflect a vision that you have that can be expansive enough to be God-glorifying, yet realistic.

4. List a typical committee agenda for a committee that you are involved in. How much of this is internally focussed and how much is directly related to the mission? Can you identify the team members and their contribution in this setting?

5. Can you think of the ways conflict is handled within your team or congregation? How might this be improved?[76]

6. List a number of ways that proactive pastoral care can be conducted in your setting. How might you introduce one or two of these elements in your congregation?

7. Think of a crisis within your pastoral setting now and outline what is happening. The challenge is to think as deeply and carefully as you can from a variety of perspectives. What steps are being taken to address this concern? How are relationships influencing this situation, both positively and negatively? Theologically reflect on this situation and determine options for ways forward.

8. Do some research to create a list of well-respected professional practitioners in such fields as psychology, medicine, social work, and justice. Be sure to seek the advice of church leaders in your community.

CHAPTER 6

CONCLUSION

In this brief journey we have explored the basis for our *being* and *doing* in ministry and leadership. Character development and spiritual formation is the foundation. Our need to be attentive to God's communication with us requires discipline, intentionality, and courage. This is not a journey for the faint-hearted! Instead, it is an adventure directed by God and guided by his mission in his world. We are his under-shepherds, servants that become servants of the people of God. Empowering others for God's mission is always within our mutual endeavour of making Christlike disciples who, in turn, make Christlike disciples. Our calling is enabled by the gifting of God's Holy Spirit. We march to the beat of a different drum, and so the Kingdom values we express may appear counter-cultural or, at very least, counter-intuitive. Discernment is found in listening well to God through practising the spiritual disciplines and reflecting on what we hear and see. We need courage as we gain new perspectives and experiences that will inform our theological understanding. When we are committed to incarnational ministry and relationship, then our goals and strategies in ministry and leadership can honour God. A focus on people will shine through the way we conduct our administrative tasks and how we handle conflict. May God bless you in your journey of ministry and leadership. Always remember, "You are a chosen people, a royal priesthood, a holy nation, God's special possession, that you may declare the praises of him who called you out of darkness into his wonderful light. Once you were not a people, but now you are the people of God; once you had not received mercy, but now you have received mercy" (1 Peter 2:9-10).

QUESTIONS FOR REFLECTION

1. What are three key insights that you have gleaned from this book? How might these insights be incorporated into your life and ministry?

2. Read 2 Peter 1:3-11. According to this passage what are we to do in order to be fruitful and effective as Christians? What is the resource for this? Give specific actions that you can do this coming week toward this fruitfulness.

3. Read through Wesley's Covenant Renewal Service (http://www.seed-bed.com/john-wesleys-covenant-renewal-service-today) and prayerfully consider the words of confession and recommitment. Wesley's Band questions can also guide your thoughts toward confession and commitment:

   1. What known sins have you committed since our last meeting?

   2. What temptations have you met with?

   3. How were you delivered?

   4. What have you thought, said, or done of which you doubt whether it be sin or not?

   5. Have you nothing you desire to keep secret?

SUGGESTION FOR FURTHER READING

Beginner

Blackaby, Henry and Richard Blackaby. *Spiritual Leadership: Moving People on to God's Agenda*. Revised. Nashville, TN: B & H Publisher, 2011.

Henderson, D. Michael. *John Wesley's Class Meeting: A Model for Making Disciples*. Nappanee, IN: Francis Asbury Press, 1997.

Leclerc, Diane and Mark A. Maddix. *Spiritual Formation: A Wesleyan Paradigm*. Kansas City, MO: Beacon Hill Press, 2011.

Maddix, Mark A. and Diane Leclerc, eds. *Pastoral Practices: A Wesleyan Paradigm*. Kansas City, MO: Beacon Hill Press, 2013.

Intermediate to Advanced

Blevins, Dean G. and Mark A. Maddix. *Discovering Discipleship: Dynamics of Christian Education.* Kansas City, MO: Beacon Hill Press, 2010.

Fairbanks, E. LeBron, Dwight M. Gunter II, and James R. Couchenour. *Best Practices for Effective Boards.* Kansas City, MO: Beacon Hill Press, 2012.

Northouse, Peter G. *Leadership: Theory and Practice.* 7th edition. Los Angeles, CA: Sage, 2016.

Smith, James K. A. *You Are What You Love: The Spiritual Power of Habit.* Grand Rapids, MI: Brazos Press, 2016.

Warner, Marcus and Hans Finzel. *Rare Leadership: 4 Uncommon Habits for Increasing Trust, Joy and Engagement in the People You Lead.* Chicago, IL: Moody Publishers, 2016.

ENDNOTES

1   Colin Brown, ed. *The New International Dictionary of Theology,* Volume 3 (Grand Rapids: Zondervan, 1986), 544.

2   Art Lindsley, "The Priesthood of All Believers," Oct 15, 2013, found at https://tifwe.org/resource/the-priesthood-of-all-believers, accessed July 5, 2017.

3   John Maxwell, *Developing the Leader Within You* (Nashville: Thomas Nelson Publisher, 1993), 1.

4   Henry Blackaby & Richard Blackaby, *Spiritual Leadership: Moving People onto God's Agenda* (Nashville: B & H Publishing, 2011), 119.

5   Maxwell, *Developing the Leader,* 4.

6   James K. A. Smith, *You Are What You Love: The Spiritual Power of Habit* (Grand Rapids: Brazos Press, 2016), 90.

7   Augustine of Hippo, *Confessions*, Lib1.1-2.2.5.5: CSEL 33, 1-5.

8   Tom Wright, *The Day the Revolution Began: Rethinking the Meaning of Jesus' Crucifixion* (San Francisco: HarperOne, 2016), 86.

9   Smith, *What You Love,* 8.

10 M. Robert Mulholland, "Spiritual Formation in Christ and Mission with Christ," *Journal of Spiritual Formation & Soul Care* 6.1 (2013): 13, 15.

11 Klaus Issler, "Five Key Barriers to Deep learning and Character Formation Based Primarily on Jesus' Parable of the Four Soils," *Christian Education Journal Series* 3.9 Supplement (2012): 155.

12 Smith, *What You Love,* 9.

13 Smith, *What You Love,* 25.

14 Douglas John Hall, "Theological Education as Character Formation?" *Theological Education* Supplement I (1988): 54.

15 Bruce A Stevens, *Emotional Learning: The Way We Are Wired for Intimacy*, found at http://www.vividpublishing.com.au, accessed June 30, 2017.

16 Stephen Cherry, "Discipleship and Christian Character," *Theology* 119.3 (2016): 196.

17 Cited in Henri Nouwen, *Out of Solitude* (Notre Dame, IN: Ave Maria Press, 1974), 42.

18 United Methodist Church, http://www.umc.org/how-we-serve/the-wesleyan-means-of-grace, accessed June 15, 2017.

19 Smith, *What You Love*, 94.

20 Lectionary readings can be found at http://lectionary.library.vanderbilt.edu/lections.php?year=C&season . These give you an OT reading, NT reading, a Psalm, and a Gospel reading. Many congregations use these readings every Sunday and the preacher chooses one or more of these from which to preach.

21 Greater detail can be found on such web sites as: http://www.ignatianspirituality.com/ignatian-prayer/the-what-how-why-of-prayer/praying-with-scripture . This is just one of numerous sites that can assist in cultivating the habit of praying the Scriptures and tuning our ear to hear the voice of God.

22 Stephen Covey, *The Seven Habits of Highly Successful People* (New York: Simon & Schuster, 1989), 195-196.

23 Covey, *Seven Habits*, 195-196.

24 Martin E. Marty, "Trust as The Virtue for Ministry," *Reflective Practice: Formation and Supervision in Ministry* 32 (2012): 10-21.

25 Adopted from Richard Barrett, *Building Trust in Your Team*, found at https://richardbarrettblog.net/2014/04/11/building-trust-in-your-team-the-trust-matrix/, accessed June 16, 2017.

26 Brené Brown, *The Anatomy of Trust*, found at www.willowgroveadventist.org/file/download/1031, accessed June 19, 2017)

27 D. Michael Henderson, *John Wesley's Class Meetings: A Model for Making Disciples* (Wilmore, KY: Rafiki Books, 2016), 96, 98.

28 Henderson, *John Wesley's Class Meetings*, 99.

29 Henderson, *John Wesley's Class Meetings*, 101.

30 Steven Hitlin, "Values as the Core of Personal Identity: Drawing Links between Two Theories of Self," *Social Psychology Quarterly* 66.2 (2003): 118-37.

31 Aubury Malphurs *Values-Driven Leadership: Discovering and Developing Your Core Values for Ministry* (Grand Rapids: Baker, 2004), 31-44.

32 Lovett H. Weems, *Leadership in the Wesleyan Spirit* (Nashville: Abingdon Press, 1999), 13, 21, 34, 44.

33 Lenny Luchetti, "Theological Empathy and John Wesley's Missional Field Preaching," *Great Commission Research Journal* 8.2 (2017): 181.

34 Blackaby & Blackaby, *Spiritual Leadership*, 160.

[35] Greenleaf is quoted in Peter G. Northouse, *Leadership Theory and Practice* 7th Edition (Thousand Oaks, CA: SAGE Publications, 2016), 226.

[36] Ken Bible, *Wesley Hymns* (Kansas City, MO: Lillenas Publishing Co., 1982), A-7.

[37] Alan Hirsch, found at http://www.theforgottenways.org/apest/, accessed June 28, 2017. See also, Alan Hirsch, *The Forgotten Ways* (Grand Rapids: Brazos Press, 2006).

[38] Ruth Haley Barton, *Strengthening the Soul of Your Leadership* (Downers Grove: InterVarsity Press, 2012), 76.

[39] Bruce G Allder, *A Hope Filled Journey Under His Sky* (Eugene, OR: Resource Publications, 2016), 23-25. The wider account of BJ's life also traces the formative and "raw" material that made BJ an amazingly effective missionary in Thailand and South-East Asia. It fits Barton's understanding of God creating us with the proclivities that are the indicators of a calling.

[40] This is not the place to spend time working through the discernment of God's will; however, this is an important task for the leader to do. An old but tried and tested book is Garry Friesen, *Decision Making & the Will of God.* (Portland, OR: Multnomah Press, 1980).

[41] Church of the Nazarene, *Manual 2013–2017: History, Constitution, Government, Ritual* (Kansas City: Nazarene Publishing House, 2013), paragraphs 527-532.2; 226-231.4

[42] Neville Emslie, "Transformative Learning and Ministry Formation," *Journal of Adult Theological Education,* 13.1 (2016): 48-63, gives a good account of the transformative process that can take place as a person encounters a disruptive event and works through to integrate a new perspective.

[43] Robert L. Kinast, *Let Ministry Teach: A Guide to Theological Reflection* (Collegeville, MN: The Liturgical Press, 1996), xiii.

[44] Lynne M. Baab, *The Power of Listening: Building Skills for Mission and Ministry* (Lanham, MD: Rowman & Littlefield, 2014), loc. 318 of 2963.

[45] Northouse, *Leadership,* 46, gives a good summary of many leadership approaches outlining their relative strengths and weakness.

[46] http://www.educational-business-articles.com/leadership-versus-management/, accessed June 27, 2017.

47 Adopted and adapted from Tom Nees, *Reflections from Tom Nees on Leadership, Compassion and Justice*, found at www.tomnees.com, accessed July 3, 2017.

48 Thomas Sergiovanni, *Moral Leadership: Getting to the Heart of School Improvement* (San Francisco: Jossey Bass, 1991).

49 William Barclay. *The Gospel of Matthew: Volume 1*, Revised Edition (Philadelphia, Westminster Press: 1975), 88.

50 Barclay, *Gospel of Matthew*, 96.

51 Smith, *What You Love*, 77.

52 Josh Butler, "Census 2016: Australia Is Bigger, Older, More Diverse, found at http://www.huffingtonpost.com.au/2017/06/26/census-2016-australia-is-bigger-older-more-diverse_a_23003168/, accessed July 5, 2017.

53 Gregory Spencer, "Time is Up and Space is Down," *Journal of Spiritual Formation & Soul Care* 10.1 (2017): 106.

54 Spencer, "Time is Up," 109.

55 Spencer, "Time is Up," 113.

56 Allder, *A Hope Filled Journey*, 54. See chapters 3 & 4 for an extended example of "walking slowly" with people and the amazing effectiveness of this approach.

57 Allder, *A Hope Filled Journey*, 75.

58 C. Christopher Smith & John Pattison, *Slow Church: Cultivating Community in the Patient Way of Jesus* (Downers Grove, InterVarsity Press, 2014), 44-61.

59 Baab, *The Power of Listening*, loc. 142 of 2963.

60 Paul D. Borden, *Hit the Bullseye: How Denominations Can Aim the Congregation at the Mission Field* (Nashville, Abingdon, 2003), 39.

61 E. LeBron Fairbanks, Dwight M. Gunter, James R. Couchenour, *Best Practices for Effective Boards* (Kansas City, MO: Beacon Hill Press, 2012), 121.

62 Aubury Malphurs. *Values-Driven Leadership: Discovering and Developing Your Core Values for Ministry* (Grand Rapids: Baker, 2004), 55.

63 Peter Greer & Chris Horst, *Mission Drift: The Unspoken Crisis Facing Leaders, Charities, & Churches.* (Grand Rapids: Baker, 2015).

64 I recommend: Northouse, *Leadership*; Larry Osborne, *Sticky Teams: Keeping Your Leadership Team and Staff on the Same Page* (Grand Rapid: Zondervan, 2010); Stephen A. Macchia, *Becoming a Healthy Team: Five*

Traits of Vital Leadership (Lexington, MA: Leadership Transformations, 2013).

[65] Macchia, *Becoming a Healthy Team.*

[66] Northouse, *Leadership*, 368-371.

[67] Tom Rath, *Strengths Finder 2.0*, found at www.strengths.gallup.com, accessed July 18, 2017.

[68] Patrick Lencioni, *The Ideal Team Player: How to Recognise and Cultivate the Three Essential Virtues* (Hoboken, NJ: Jossey-Bass, 2016).

[69] Houston E. Thompson, *Conflict Management for Faith Leaders* (Kansas City, MO: Beacon Hill Press, 2014), 22.

[70] I recommend Craig E. Runde & Tim A. Flanagan, *Becoming a Conflict Competent Leader: How You and Your Organization Can Manage Conflict Effectively* (San Francisco, CA: Jossey-Bass, 2013).

[71] Thompson, *Conflict Management*, chapters 5-10.

[72] Barbara A. Budjac Corvette, *Conflict Management: A Practical Guide to Developing Negotiation Strategies,* (Essex: Pearson Education Ltd. 2014), 36.

[73] Adopted from Corvette, *Conflict Management*, 37.

[74] Runde & Flanagan, *Becoming a Conflict Competent Leader*, 235.

[75] Eugene H. Peterson, *Working the Angles: The Shape of Pastoral Integrity* (Grand Rapids: Eerdmans, 1994), 4.

FRAMEWORKS FOR LAY LEADERSHIP

ABOUT THE EDITOR

Rob A. Fringer, PhD–Principal and lecturer in Biblical Studies and Biblical Language at Nazarene Theological College in Brisbane. Rob is an ordained elder in the Church of the Nazarene and has 15 years of pastoral experience working in the areas of Youth, Adult Discipleship, and Community Outreach. He is co-author of *Theology of Luck: Fate, Chaos, & Faith* and *The Samaritan Project* both published by Beacon Hill Press of Kansas City. Rob is married (Vanessa) and has two children (Sierra and Brenden).

BOOKS IN THE
FRAMEWORKS FOR LAY LEADERSHIP SERIES

ENGAGING THE STORY OF GOD
Rob A. Fringer

EXPLORING A WESLEYAN THEOLOGY
David B. McEwan

EMBODYING A THEOLOGY OF MINISTRY AND LEADERSHIP
Bruce G. Allder

ENTERING THE MISSION OF GOD
Richard Giesken

EXPRESSING A NAZARENE IDENTITY
Floyd Cunningham

EMBRACING A DOCTRINE OF HOLINESS
David B. McEwan and Rob A. Fringer